CRITICAL ESSAYS IN MODERN LITERATURE

CRITICAL ESSAYS IN MODERN LITERATURE

The Fiction and Criticism of Katherine Anne Porter (revised)
Harry James Mooney, Jr.

Entrances to Dylan Thomas' Poetry
Ralph Maud

The Fiction of J. D. Salinger (revised)
Frederick L. Gwynn and Joseph L. Blotner

Chronicles of Conscience: A Study of George Orwell and Arthur Koestler
Jenni Calder

Richard Wright: An Introduction to the Man and His Work
Russell Carl Brignano

The Hole in the Fabric: Science, Contemporary Literature, and Henry James
Strother B. Purdy

Tragic Realism and Modern Society: Studies in the Sociology of the Modern Novel
John Orr

Reading the Thirties: Texts and Contexts
Bernard Bergonzi

The Romantic Genesis of the Modern Novel
Charles Schug

The Great Succession: Henry James and the Legacy of Hawthorne
Robert Emmet Long

The Plays and Novels of Peter Handke
June Schlueter

Yeats, Eliot, Pound and the Politics of Poetry: Richest to the Richest
Cairns Craig

After Innocence: Visions of the Fall in Modern Literature
Terry Otten

The Metafictional Muse: The Works of Robert Coover, Donald Barthelme, and William H. Gass
Larry McCaffery

The Grand Continuum: Reflections on Joyce and Metaphysics
David A. White

The Grand Continuum

The Grand Continuum:

Reflections on Joyce and Metaphysics

David A. White

UNIVERSITY OF PITTSBURGH PRESS

Published by the University of Pittsburgh Press, Pittsburgh, Pa. 15260

Feffer and Simons, Inc., London
Manufactured in the United States of America

Library of Congress Cataloging in Publication Data

White, David A., 1942–
The grand continuum.

(Critical essays in modern literature)
Bibliography: p. 193
Includes index.
1. Joyce, James, 1882–1941—Philosophy. 2. Philosophy in literature. I. Title.
II. Series.
PR6019.09Z944 823'.912 82-4740
ISBN 0-8229-3803-0 AACR2

Portions of this book were originally published in "Husserl and the Poetic Consciousness," *The Personalist* 53 (1972): 408–24; and in "The Labyrinth of Language: Joyce and Wittgenstein," *James Joyce Quarterly* 12 (1975): 294–304.

We are grateful for permission to quote from the following works: *A Portrait of the Artist as a Young Man* by James Joyce, copyright 1916 by B. W. Heubsch, copyright renewed 1944 by Nora Joyce, definitive text copyright © 1964 by the Estate of James Joyce, reprinted by permission of Viking Penguin Inc., by The Society of Authors as the literary representative of the Estate of James Joyce, and by Jonathan Cape Ltd. on behalf of the Executors of the James Joyce Estate; *Ulysses* by James Joyce, copyright 1961 by Random House, Inc., and The Bodley Head; *Finnegans Wake* by James Joyce, copyright 1939 by James Joyce, copyright renewed 1967 by George Joyce and Lucia Joyce, reprinted by permission of Viking Penguin Inc. and The Society of Authors as the literary representative of the Estate of James Joyce.

To my teacher
Newton P. Stallknecht

By the light of philophosy . . .
things will begin to clear up a bit one way or another

Finnegans Wake 119.4–6

Contents

PART II. Anticipations of the Flux

PART III. Wisdom and the *Wake*

Acknowledgments

First and foremost, I would like to thank my wife, Mary Jeanne Larrabee, for her customary stellar performance as editor and advisor. I would also like to express my appreciation to Professor Roger McHugh, University College, National University of Ireland, for his helpful guidance during a tour of various Joycean haunts in Dublin. And finally a special note of thanks to the members of a class on Joyce and the philosophy of language given at the New School for Social Research in the spring term of 1978; their penetrating interest in the philosophical aspects of Joyce forced their instructor to reflect on these matters more deeply and rigorously than he might have been inclined to do otherwise.

Textual Note

All *Finnegans Wake* citations are from the Viking Press copyright 1967 edition. Citations from *Ulysses* follow the 1961 Modern Library edition, and include both page and line numbers (as in Gifford and Seidman's *Notes for Joyce*). Citations from *A Portrait of the Artist as a Young Man* are from the Viking Press copyright 1964 edition.

Introduction

Finnegans Wake, the final moment in the grand continuum of Joyce's prose work, still conceals much from those of us with minds less nimble than that of its creator. Although individual words and phrases, sometimes entire sentences, gradually become less perplexing after repeated readings, there remains the continuous struggle to detect the delicate interplay between this or that apparently impenetrable pun and the overarching structure of the work. It seems clear that any one part of this massive edifice cannot be appreciated until one achieves a firm grasp of the whole. Yet it seems equally clear that knowledge of the whole depends on discerning the various meanings packed into each part. A classic interpretive circle results, next to impossible to escape, given the apparent boundlessness of the circle described. And yet the magnitude of the interpreter's task has not restricted critical attempts to shed some light on the vastness of that continuum. This study is another such attempt.

My approach to Joyce is marked both by humility and by hubris. The humility results from the fact that I have adopted only one of the many possible critical perspectives on the world of the *Wake.* So much for humility; as for hubris, the perspective I wish to explore concerns an introduction to the major philosophical themes which underlie the narrative structure of the *Wake*. Furthermore, I attempt to extend this philosophical dimension to include the relevant aspects of *A Portrait of the Artist as a Young Man* and *Ulysses*. Thus the grand continuum in my title refers both to *Finnegans Wake* as an autonomous whole and to all of Joyce's full-length prose writings. For purposes of this study, I have assumed a break of sorts between *Dubliners*, brief yet moving stories starkly drawn, and the distinctive metaphysical continuum that followed Joyce's early effort. My premise is that the *Wake* portrays an Olympian vision of language and reality which originated with *Portrait* and was developed with great power and scope in *Ulysses*.

My concern here is not to rival the various admirable studies comparing Joyce to a particular figure in the history of philosophy, such as Aristotle, Aquinas, Bruno, or Kierkegaard. Rather it is to derive a coherent and comprehensive metaphysics which is peculiarly Joycean both in texture and structure and which sustains the major prose works despite their stylistic diversity. My defense against the charge of hubris is that this study is intended to be introductory both in the selection of philosophical themes (which may well be incomplete) and the ordering of those themes (which may perhaps distort somewhat their ultimate importance). But despite the risk of failing to reach my goals, I must attempt such an inquiry to invite serious Joyceans to pursue this neglected aspect of Joyce's work.

Finnegans Wake serves as the focal point for this study, since in it Joyce explicitly asserts a variegated metaphysical position. However, the *Wake*'s relative metaphysical maturity can also constitute a backdrop for an excursus into the language of both *Portrait* and *Ulysses*. An examination of the two major prose works preceding the *Wake* should indicate the extent to which Joyce had been concerned with some of the same philosophical themes and with some of the stylistic techniques for dealing with these themes in a work of imaginative literature. The metaphysical boundaries described by the *Wake* include important stylistic aspects of these two earlier works, aspects which may remain relatively unappreciated unless seen with the "hindsight" provided by knowledge of the *Wake*. Furthermore, we may also recognize that the metaphysics of the *Wake* was not a hybrid work of artifice constructed just for purposes of ordering one work.

Any serious student of Joyce should want to understand the metaphysical structure of *Finnegans Wake,* at least to some degree. And this intention need not spring from an intrinsic interest in metaphysics. After all, it is more than plausible to assume that Joyce's work is more literary than philosophical. But part of the purpose of this study will be to suggest that some of the difficulties in understanding the *Wake* as literature depend on the ramifications of the metaphysical structure ordering the *Wake* as a whole. Thus one reason why even the most indefatigable reader of the *Wake* becomes disoriented is that the usually stable metaphysics which tacitly grounds the language of traditional fiction is different from the metaphysics defining the world of the *Wake.* As a result, a concerted attempt to understand the purely metaphysical components of the *Wake*'s language should contribute to apprehending the *Wake* as a unified literary whole. We may not understand every syllable of the *Wake* after completing such an investigation, but it would surely be an advance to know that our continued lack of success might have something to do with abstract problems resulting from metaphysical tensions oscillating at the *Wake*'s very core. The more time and effort spent in appreciating the importance of the Wake's metaphysical structure, the less remote and esoteric will be the reasons why the uniquely concrete language of the *Wake* takes the forms that it does.

I should perhaps also stress that my approach will concentrate on locating and describing the comprehensive metaphysical structure of *Finnegans Wake* rather than on a detailed interpretive account of its endless nooks and crannies. In no way can a critical discussion of this sort do justice to the immeasurable richness of detail in the *Wake*'s language. Nor is it possible to connect this complex structure to the various thematic accounts of the *Wake* already existing in the secondary literature, since such an attempt would bloat this study almost beyond measure. The most that can be hoped for is that selective treatment of an essential core of the work will help to illuminate a whole of apparently limitless dimension. I am convinced that the metaphysical structure to be described, even though it has been elicited from a relatively small number of passages, will be sufficiently ample to accommodate almost any part of that whole which a persistent reader may wish to locate within it.

My principal guide for determining the structure of this metaphysics has been the finished texts of the major prose works. I have also consulted Joyce's letters, the excellent biographical studies, and the reconstructions of earlier versions of the *Wake,* since students of Joyce, especially of *Finnegans Wake,* obviously need all the help they can get. However, the kind of systematic investigation pursued in this study must ultimately be based on the texts themselves rather than on sources which are essential for other types of critical inquiry.

I have attempted to develop the foundational concepts of this metaphysics as rigorously as the fluid language of the *Wake* permits. But "rigorous" is not intended to be a synonym for rigor mortis. I hope that the description of these concepts does not sound too austere for readers interested in this aspect of Joyce, but perhaps unfamiliar with the technical terminology and content of metaphysical thought. The sympathetic reader should look on this study as an essay in philosophical appreciation of a series of literary masterpieces, couched in language at times unavoidably reflecting the abstract character of what Joyce is saying.

One last word: to take *Finnegans Wake* seriously as a metaphysical document may strike some as, at best, an exercise in misplaced concreteness and, at worst, sheer insanity. However, I believe that the more seriously we study the metaphysical dimension of the *Wake,* the more reliable will be the final judgment that the *Wake* is just the "hoax that joke bilked," especially if it should turn out that this dimension is simply another wing of that hoax, and thus no less or more important than any other wing. If, however, we do not look at and think about the *Wake* as its complex panoply demands, then in the final analysis the hoax may be on us.

My opening chapter situates the abstract character of the *Wake*'s metaphysics within a hermeneutical context appropriate for a work of literature. Certain objections to the type of interpretation advanced here are posed and answered as a preparation for what follows. My study is divided into three parts of two chapters each: I—In the Wake of Metaphysics; II—Anticipations of the Flux; III—Wisdom and the *Wake.* The first part contains a systematic recapitulation of the principal metaphysical notions found in the *Wake,* and the specific stylistic techniques employed in the *Wake* as related to their function in evoking the unique metaphysical directives underlying these techniques. Part II details the relevant connections linking, respectively, *Portrait* and *Ulysses* to the metaphysical structure outlined in part I. The third part comments on the sense in which the tensions arising from the *Wake*'s metaphysics pertain to the problems of understanding and interpreting the *Wake* as a purely literary vehicle, and concludes with a chapter in which the Joycean metaphysics will be placed in apposition to representative selections drawn from the work of two prominent twentieth-century philosophers—Ludwig Wittgenstein and Edmund Husserl. The resulting comparisons will illuminate both Joyce as metaphysician and also those philosophers as professional inquirers into the complexities of human consciousness.

The Grand Continuum

Some Principles of Interpretation

The importance of the philosophical dimension in Joyce's work, especially in understanding *Finnegans Wake,* should not require any special apology. No less a Joycean than Anthony Burgess prefaces his summary remarks about his treatment of the *Wake* (in the concluding chapter of *ReJoyce*) by noting that he felt "forced to ignore much that is important—the metaphysics, for instance, that is personified in the characters."[1] Thus one of the most perceptive students of Joyce has forthrightly acknowledged the critical relevance of the metaphysics embodied in the *Wake,* making a conciliatory bow toward philosophy which may be found repeated by others confronting the more abstract features of Joyce's most complex writing. The fact that Burgess himself has retreated from elucidating the details of this metaphysical structure should also bear witness to the intrinsic difficulty of this type of critical endeavor.

Burgess speaks of the metaphysics in the *Wake* rather than of a fully ornamented philosophy, and the distinction between the two is worth keeping in mind throughout this study. Metaphysics, traditionally understood as the most regal branch of philosophy, normally is characterized by both abstract concepts and diffuse forms of argumentation in the development of those concepts. It is this area of philosophy, the most fundamental and therefore the most important, which will orient the following study.

Many philosophers are named in the *Wake*, some more directly and more frequently than others—for example, Nicholas of Cusa, Giordano Bruno, and above all, Giambattista Vico. But of course the mere mention of these names does not transform the *Wake* into a literary work with a palpably metaphysical character. Motion and rest, space and time, identity and difference, cause and effect—these concepts are the stuff of metaphysics, and the extent to which the *Wake* incorporates these and related concepts is the extent to which it may be said to possess a working metaphysics. And incorporate them it certainly does. At times, one must temper the fine edge of humor and irony in the *Wake* somewhat in order to sense the pressure of Joyce's language as an instrument of metaphysical temper. But once this abstract perspective has been allowed to emerge, the resulting metaphysical position becomes relatively clear and coherent, occasionally compelling, and always bold. And its importance, hinted at by Burgess and others, will assume a fitting prominence as this study unfolds.[2]

Those familiar with the general contours of Joycean criticism will perhaps have reservations about a study of this sort. These reservations may be stated in the form of three questions, each militating in a different way against construing *Finnegans Wake* (as I do) as a literary work animated by a discernible and vital metaphysical structure. First, what indications, whether through style or in content, point to the real presence of a metaphysics underlying the *Wake?* Second, many critics believe that because the *Wake* exhibits many of the unconscious characteristics of a dream, its language need have little if any relevance to the relatively ordered appearance of waking life. Why then should the *Wake*, its complexities as a literary dream manifest to all, be scrutinized according to the dictates of metaphysics, an interpretive rubric which can apply to a dream only in the most marginal sense? And third, given that the *Wake* is a work pervaded by humor, how can the buoyancy of humor and the seriousness of philosophical metaphysics be compatible?

When examined carefully and critically, the premises behind these questions soon vanish as threats to our projected study. In fact, determining exactly why these premises are insufficient will indirectly provide a justification for actively pursuing the critical interpretation I have proposed. Three questions will now be developed and analyzed.

Metaphysics in the *Wake*

Finnegans Wake begins with the word "riverrun." The rich significance of this particular curtain-raiser has not gone unnoticed, especially in the critical literature. One easily discerns that "riverrun" combines the noun "river" with the verb "run" into a single neologism. Now this type of compound is not new to Joyce's style; already in *Portrait* words such as "sootcoated" (115), "softworded" (155), "hazewrapped" (169), "fireconsumed" (177), "gustblown" (192), and a number of others had made an appearance. What then is the special significance of "riverrun"? Why should it now contribute to, and partially define, the presence of a metaphysical dimension? The answer rests on an intimate and extended encounter with the *Wake* as a whole, not simply on intuiting eccentricities in its first word. Nevertheless, a hint pointing the way toward subsequent inquiry may be found by recalling that "riverrun" has also been construed by some *Wake* readers as a pun on "reverend." Yet surely this meaning has little if anything to do with the primarily liquid significance of "riverrun." How can this connotative range be possible for a single word?

The word "riverrun" represents a challenge which one cannot evade simply by regarding it as an esoteric illustration of how words assume significance in literary contexts. For in order to understand the full complexity of Joyce's innovative language, we must appreciate the sense in which notions and principles embodied in classical metaphysics have been woven into the fabric of the *Wake*. This study will show how a locution such as "riverrun"—and similar linguistic maneuvers of varying degrees of complexity—can be more adequately understood when the *Wake* has been located within a coherent metaphysical structure including within its scope the relation between language as such and all that is other than language. Those averse to the abstract rigors of metaphysics might appeal to the *Wake*'s almost prosaic injunction: "Let us leave theories there and return to here's here" (76.10). The point is, however, that if "here's here" should include both a river running and a reverend concurrently, then precisely where is "here's here"? If "here" means the letter of the *Wake*'s language, or if "here" represents an understanding of what the *Wake* intends to accomplish, then it may well be necessary to explore a few "theories" before returning to the *Wake* as it stands.

"Riverrun" is metaphysically significant in several ways. First, it combines a substantive reference to a type of thing with a verbal reference to a primary property of that thing, thus tending to collapse within the limits of one word the traditionally held metaphysical distinction between an entity and a property of that entity. Second, and from a more abstract perspective, the word evokes the conjunction of stability and movement. And this interplay of opposites, the stability of the river sliding into the movement of the river running, subtly but ineluctably introduces a much more cosmic metaphysical confrontation. As the initial word of the *Wake*, "riverrun" must be taken to indicate where the narrative begins. As such, it may appear that prior to "riverrun" nothing exists. But there is a small orthographic clue to the careful reader that the *Wake* has not been ordered according to standard literary conventions: its first word is uncapitalized, as if a sentence had been interrupted in mid-thought. And of course this turns out to be precisely the case. For what precedes "riverrun" is not an extraliterary silence, but "A way a lone a last a loved a long the"—the apparently unfinished concluding sentence of the *Wake*. The perceptive reader who wonders why the word "riverrun" is uncapitalized on page 3 and why the *Wake*'s final sentence on page 628 lacks concluding punctuation (not to mention a verb) will connect these two very distant narrative components. This reader would then realize, in one of those insights which may cause as much pain as pleasure, that the *Wake* has been constructed as a circle of immense circumference, a circle which invites if not compels the reader to continue reading forever. Just as the initial inscribing of a visible circle must start somewhere, "riverrun" merely marks the onset of the *Wake*'s uniquely eternal motion.

This remarkable narrative circularity suggests that the events described in the *Wake* will recur as many times as the circuit of that narrative is traced by an individual reader. Given this stylistic peculiarity, it should not be surprising that the sequence of events endlessly recurring in the narrative receives metaphysical amplification and indeed justification within the very narration of those events. The presence of the philosopher of history, Vico, naturally looms large here, although in the final analysis perhaps no larger than that of other philosophers who may not appear so immediately pertinent. But it is essential to note for now that this narrative circularity can be deduced from a careful reading of the purely formal textual features just outlined. We need not know anything about Vico's thought to be aware of the *Wake*'s circular structure (although some knowledge of Viconian principles of historical cycles would doubtless enrich one's understanding of some of the metaphysical considerations involved).[3]

This point increases in importance as soon as its implications are brought into the open. If, for example, the circular structure of the *Wake* mirrors geometrical circularity, then it would follow that "riverrun" is no more the first word of *Finnegans Wake* than any other word in the work—a circle does not admit of starting (or ending) points and neither would a literary work with an avowedly circular form. In theory, one could begin with *any* word in the *Wake* and eventually pick up the circular thread of the work's narrative. This particular inference, although somewhat legitimate, should clearly not be pressed too far. Presumably the fact that Joyce made the *Wake* begin as it does on page 3 and follow a certain sequence until it ends on page 628 has a certain interpretive significance. Nevertheless, I suggest that this formal characteristic at least allows us to move around the

Wake as if the entire work were present all at once, just as a circle is so present, without subverting the essential quality of the narrative sequence. Thus elements may be selected from any location in the *Wake* and then ordered according to the dictates of the interpretive scheme adopted.

Yet even more consequential implications follow from the circular structure of the *Wake*. Because the narrative of the *Wake* never stops and never starts, the *Wake* is also defined by continuous semantic motion. Rest, the classic antithesis of motion, enters the picture only from an extraliterary source, that is, when the reader decides to halt the perpetual sweep of the narrative at some point. It is important to note, however, that such continuous motion applies only to the *Wake* as a complete narrative sequence; it would not necessarily follow that the specific referential content of the *Wake*'s narrative must also be defined by continuous motion. The presence of this type of formal motion should nonetheless alert us to the possibility that the same sort of fundamental motion may also be present in the content of the *Wake*.

Another consequence may also be noted. For if the referential content of the *Wake* is in continuous motion (as hinted at by its formal structure), with no beginning and no end, then the classical divisions of time—past, present, future—lose their powers of differentiation. The relations of "before" and "after" become meaningless if what is understood from one possible perspective as "before" can also be understood from an equally possible perspective as "after." Thus whatever temporality has been incorporated into the narrative of the *Wake* will differ, perhaps quite radically, from temporality as traditionally conceived. The precise nature of its structure, if indeed time in the *Wake* has a structure, must be established gradually, by observing how the various episodes constituting the circular narrative are related to one another.

The formal characteristic of circularity thus displays definite metaphysical overtones, and if substantive metaphysical consequences also animate the *Wake*'s content, then there should be more than sufficient reason to approach and scrutinize the work from that standpoint. However, we should be careful to identify as precisely as possible what we are seeking. For example, determining the most appropriate way to look for this metaphysics is itself a problem. For although many philosophers and metaphysical notions are named in the *Wake,* we can infer little from this fact alone. Consider this passage: "marx my word fort, for a chip off the old Flint, (in the Nichtian glossery which purveys aprioric roots for aposteriorious tongues this is nat language at any sinse of the world . . .)" (83.10–12). Two and possibly three names of philosophers are punned on here—Marx, Nietzsche (and perhaps Fichte if "Nichtian" also encompasses Fichtean); in addition, the juxtaposition of "aprioric" and "aposteriorious" clearly refers to one of the fundamental distinctions in Kant's *Critique of Pure Reason.* But should we assume from these references that any of the doctrines of these philosophers constitute an essential element in the *Wake*'s metaphysical structure? If so, which doctrines? Furthermore, assuming that we could derive both Nietzschean and Kantian positions from various texts in the *Wake,* could these doctrines be developed with mutual compatibility (since we know, for example, that Nietzsche habitually referred to the sage of Königsberg as "old" Kant and harshly criticized many of his teachings)?

One might object that such questions are artificial, since their context is defined exclusively by German philosophers and metaphysical doctrines; after all, it is well known that Italian philosophers make the *Wake* go round, in particular Vico and Bruno. But is the phrase "our wholemole millwheeling vicociclometer" (614.27) by itself any more indicative of the intrinsic importance of Vico to the *Wake*'s metaphysical structure than a similarly complex pun on another philosopher or philosophical doctrine? And to the response that references to Vico outnumber references to other philosophers, such as those of Germanic origin, we may wonder whether (a) the number of references by itself constitutes a significant factor in determining the content of the *Wake*'s metaphysics, and (b) even if sheer quantity were adopted as a criterion, would we also infer that Bruno was in fact four times as important to the *Wake* as Vico, since the number of references to Bruno is almost quadruple the number of references to Vico?[4]

Now I suggest that determining the underlying metaphysical structure of the *Wake* should begin by minimizing the importance of individual historical figures and their theories. In short, we should concentrate on what and how something is said—not on who said it. A distinction should thus be drawn between language which puns on the name of a philosopher ("Harrystotalies," 110.17), or a branch of philosophy ("epistlemadethemology," 374.17), or a philosophical concept ("aposteriorious tongues," 83.11) and language which represents, with or without puns, metaphysical principles or concepts which, upon examination, may be seen to apply to the *Wake* as a whole. Since only the language of the latter sort will exhibit the required universality, then only this language should be considered as embodying potential metaphysical pronouncements.

This interpretive principle has several important consequences. First, the detail of the resulting metaphysical structure will be constructed on the basis of what the *Wake* itself explicitly says. This metaphysics should then be sufficiently expansive to accommodate the ultimate significance of any passage in the *Wake,* although space limitations will not allow testing such comprehensiveness with anything resembling empirical completeness. But I believe that the number of texts analyzed in part I should attest to the general reliability and critical relevance of the structure elicited.

The second consequence is that the meaning of the metaphysics derived from the *Wake*'s language will be based on the assumption that the *Wake* constitutes an autonomous literary and philosophical world. In other words, the final authority for metaphysical legitimacy in the *Wake* comes not from Vico, Bruno, Aristotle, Nietzsche, Marx, Kant, or whoever else may be textually present, but from the system of thought circumscribed by the conceptual limits of the language of the *Wake* itself. If, for example, we were to initiate an analysis of the

Wake's metaphysics by postulating that Vico's philosophy will order every metaphysical element discernible in the *Wake*, then we risk destroying the interior symmetry and unity of that metaphysics. It is preferable, I suggest, to maintain a certain interpretive neutrality by assuming, at least at the start, that no one philosopher appearing in the *Wake* is any more important than any other. By so doing, we shall be alert for any passage which possesses the requisite universality and metaphysical force, regardless of where that passage occurs on the narrative circle or who may have been its original spokesman. The order that results after the elements have been gathered and deployed should represent the metaphysical structure of the *Wake* as defined by the *Wake* itself—not by any metaphysical doctrines which appear in isolated references rather than as structurally defining the whole.

As we shall see, the metaphysically significant passages are relatively few in number, spaced at irregular intervals, and generally left without explicit development by Joyce with respect to their place in the *Wake* as a whole. These factors combine so as to compel the student of the *Wake* to treat the texts with special care in order to appreciate their proper focus and scope. Thus we must understand that we are in the presence of a world defined, in part, by what Joyce has borrowed from a number of philosophers. He may not have understood them, of if he did, may have altered their positions in order to meet the demands of his own work. But in either case, our analysis of the metaphysics of the *Wake* should not be bound by the relation between, for example, what the *Wake* has Vico say and what Vico himself "really" said.

Let me amplify this last claim. Even if it could be demonstrated by the accepted procedures of scholarship that the Vico of the *Wake* is a caricature of the authentic Vico, would such a demonstration necessarily vitiate the *Wake*'s overall metaphysical significance? Is the *Wake* any less potent because its author has constructed it with concepts which only approximate the intentions of their original spokesman? Surely not. For it is just as possible that these concepts have been so adapted and integrated with other elements (including the concepts of other philosophers) that the notional ingredients have become metamorphosed into a new whole. Otherwise stated, it does not follow that the more we know about Vico (et al.), the more we know about the substantive metaphysics of the *Wake.* What Joyce *should* have said in developing the thought of philosopher *X* is not strictly relevant; we want to know what and how Joyce *did* develop the thought of philosopher *X* in order to structure *Finnegans Wake* as he wanted it. The *Wake* thus sets its own rules for establishing the metaphysical meaning of what it has borrowed from the history of thought. The structure of this metaphysics must be discerned by working from within the *Wake,* not by importing principles of scholarly correctness from disciplines which, as applied to the *Wake,* may remain external to its concerns.

One might nonetheless contend that even if the *Wake* does contain allusions to metaphysical notions, or perhaps even episodes defined by metaphysical principles, it would not necessarily follow that the presence of these parts should structure the whole. Why should we assume that metaphysics provides a global perspective on the *Wake?* And, second, why should we also assume that the metaphysics of the *Wake,* granted its existence, is both systematic and coherent?

These questions are obviously important, and I will answer them by commenting on a claim made by Anthony Burgess. Burgess asserts that in direct contrast to *Ulysses,* the *Wake* is defined by a single kind of language.[5] No one would deny that *Ulysses* has many styles, but precisely how would the one kind of language in the *Wake* be described? Surely not by the mere preponderance of puns, for there are many passages in the work without puns. Unfortunately, Burgess does not elaborate, so we are left to our own devices. Note, however, that regardless of how this stylistic unity might be analyzed, Burgess's claim implies that an apparently heterogeneous mass is in fact defined by a certain universality. In this case, of course, the universality pertains solely to form and it would be rash to assume that a formal unity of style implies an equivalent unity of content, especially that aspect of content defined by metaphysical considerations. But the point worth emphasizing here is that if the *Wake* does have a unity of style, as Burgess contends, then it is at least possible that it also has a unity of content. We can reach a verdict on this possibility only after examining the text.

My own conviction is that Burgess is basically correct. But I would also insist that the most compelling reason for ascribing such uniformity of style to the *Wake* depends primarily upon the presence of a remarkably unified metaphysics (a position with which Burgess may or may not agree). Thus we must determine whether or not a metaphysics is really present to the *Wake*.

This study will attempt to demonstrate both the content and the coherence of this metaphysics, and also to show that an essential connection exists between the content of this structure and the purely linguistic medium, the style, which brings this structure into life as a flowing literary universe. Once the elements of this metaphysics have been uncovered, we shall see that the style of the *Wake* assumes the shape that it does precisely because of the metaphysics of the *Wake*. From this perspective, then, metaphysics takes priority over style. The *Wake* reads as it does because the world represented by the *Wake* is metaphysically structured in a certain way. Thus the *Wake* can be said to have one style because that style in all its variegated richness reflects the structure of *one* metaphysical vision, a complex vision unified by coherently stated and developed concepts and principles. All stylistic variations will then serve to illustrate this complexity, their respective differences controlled by the unifying principles of the metaphysics taken as a systematic whole. Some stylistic devices will accentuate some features of this metaphysics, other devices will accentuate others. But the total range of linguistic maneuvering will be circumscribed by a single sweeping metaphysical horizon, although discerning its features will be difficult. It may be prudent at this point to dwell upon some words of wisdom drawn from the *Wake;* "Now patience; and remember patience is the great thing, and above all things else we must avoid anything like being or becoming out of patience" (108.8–10).

Metaphysics and the *Wake* as Dream

Anthony Burgess makes his case for reading the *Wake* as if it were basically constituted by the language of dreams: "After the exploration of the pre-verbal conscious mind, and even the odd trip to the borders of "sleep" which Joyce had accomplished in *Ulysses*, Burgess asks, "What can Joyce do next?" His answer: "He can only plunge straight into the unconscious mind and, for the purpose of describing it, create something like a new language."[6] But Joyce is not concerned simply with a linguistic exploration of the "unconscious mind" for its own sake; rather, his aim "is the creation of a universal myth, to which all cultures and languages are relevant" (p. 183). And the technique Joyce employs is, for Burgess, dream language, a language which "often deliberately conceals things from us" and which "must appear to us as strange, almost gibberish" (p. 189). Nevertheless, Burgess insists that we must ask what the dream is about: "Life, yes, but whose life? The answer is: the life of the whole human race—in a word, history" (p. 190). And as for the identity of the dreamer of this colossal dream? "The obvious answer is: Joyce himself, since only Joyce knows all that Joyce knows" (p. 192).

My discussion of Burgess's position is based on two questions: (1) Can the *Wake* be read as if it were a literal transcription of a dream? (2) What implications does the dream element have for analyzing the metaphysics of the *Wake?* Although my remarks are aimed primarily at Burgess's argument, they are intended to cover the overall critical approach he represents. Other accounts based on this line of interpretation will differ more in detail than in substance from Burgess's position.[7]

(1) The *Wake* can be read as if it were a dream, or even a narrative constituted by dream language, only if a number of important qualifications are granted. Consider this reflection on "a quite everydaylooking stamped addressed envelope":

> Admittedly it is an outer husk: its face, in all its featureful perfection of imperfection, is its fortune: it exhibits only the civil or military clothing of whatever passionpallid nudity or plaguepurple nakedness may happen to tuck itself under its flap. Yet to concentrate solely on the literal sense or even the psychological content of any document to the sore neglect of the enveloping facts themselves circumstantiating it is just as hurtful to sound sense (and let it be added to the truest taste) . . . (109.7–16)

The sentence goes on for a while, and the reader must determine the extent to which the remainder of this lengthy and slightly plaguepurple text contributes significantly to the matter at hand. Surely this is language not only from the *Wake* but about it as well. Here we are told, in straightforward and almost pedantic English prose, that the text "of any document" is something more than its "literal sense" or even its "psychological content." Joyce himself is warning us that a reductionist approach to the *Wake*'s language is harmful both to "sound sense" and to the "truest taste." Whether judged from a purely aesthetic perspective or according to the demands of meaning, the language of the *Wake* can be construed as emblematic of just one type of consciousness only at the cost of misreading the ultimate scope of that language.

Indeed, not just the *Wake,* but any document must be interpreted in light of the facts which circumstantiate it, all those facts which "stand around" the document under scrutiny. But how many such facts are there? And which facts are relevant to that document and which are not? If we take the hint from one of the key puns in this passage, then the number of enveloping facts which must be taken into account approaches the number of points on the circumference of a circle—infinity.

The moral seems to be that just as the meaning of a letter cannot be determined by examining only its envelope, at the same time, the meaning of something written cannot be discerned except in conjunction with whatever is "outside" it. Furthermore, there is no way to tell in advance what may or may not be relevant for elucidating a given document, an especially appropriate caveat for a document with a circular structure as expansive as that of the *Wake.* And at the forefront of our subsequent reflections on this matter should be the fact that dreams are only one type of psychological event. Consequently, this passage alone (assuming that its immediate context can be applied to the *Wake* as a whole) would suffice to hinder interpreting the *Wake* as a work which represents the "psychological content" of a dream, however extended the dimensions of that content. For this one fact about the *Wake*'s content simply cannot do justice to the full complexity of what that document envelops.

Emphasis on the dream aspect of the *Wake*'s structure is, of course, thoroughly entrenched in the secondary literature. All I want to do here is perhaps dislodge it slightly, so that we may be able to approach the *Wake* from another perspective, more complex but also, I believe, ultimately more penetrating.

Let us begin with the conclusion of Burgess's interpretation. To say that the *Wake* is a dream implies that someone dreamt it. But who? Burgess answers: the dreamer of the *Wake* is James Joyce. But as we shall see, this answer raises more problems than it solves. For since Joyce himself is not an explicit character in the work, to say that Joyce is the dreamer of the *Wake* can mean only that Joyce has dreamed the *Wake* in the process of writing it. However, surely this fact is uninformative, for it obviously holds for every written work. Even if we point to the fact that some, indeed perhaps all, of the characters in the *Wake* are aspects of Joyce's personality, to affirm that these characters have been dreamt by Joyce because Joyce created them would not distinguish between Joyce as dreamer and Joyce as author. Thus, to maintain that the *Wake* is a literary dream dreamt by Joyce, one would have to show that James Joyce is a character *in the work,* not merely indicate the undeniable fact that the work owes its existence to James Joyce.

Burgess has failed to distinguish between two different frames of reference—the external relation joining the author as conscious creator to the literary world he has created; and *within* the literary world, the relation between the meaning of the language in that world and the metaphysical status of those things language refers to. Thus Burgess has shifted illicitly from the first frame (Joyce as author *of* the *Wake*) to the second frame (Joyce as dreamer *in* the *Wake*) in order to solve the knotty problem of who dreams the *Wake.*

I conclude therefore that the *Wake* can be coherently interpreted as a dream only if there is reason to believe that each of the *Wake*'s parts is being dreamt by some character identified either within each part or elsewhere in the work. Although some might deem it worthwhile to attempt the solution of this puzzle, from the metaphysical standpoint I have adopted, the question of who dreams the *Wake* is not crucial. Let me attempt to substantiate this. Notice that simply posing the question of the identity of this dreamer as Burgess has done presupposes that the dreamer must dream the *entire* work, that is, that the *Wake* must be seen as the continuous product of a dream. But surely these related presuppositions are at odds with certain narrative details. For example, if the *Wake* is the product of a dream, then how can the following characteristics be explained?

(a) The shifts from straight prose to the language of puns —for example, "his dream monologue was over, of cause, but his drama parapolylogic had yet to be" (474.4–5). Is the language of unadorned prose just as dreamlike as the language of the puns? Surely not. And yet this conclusion seems necessary, given the premise that the *Wake* as a whole is a dream.

(b) The shifts between the language of a dream as dreamt and the prose of a narrative occurring outside the dream—such as, "from sleep we are passing" (608.33–34) and "and as I was jogging along in a dream as dozing" (404.3–4). Such shifts suggest a transition between sleep and wakefulness, but if all of the *Wake* is a dream, then this transition is impossible. The dreamer who believes he is awake remains asleep all the while.

(c) The shifts between different narrators—such as in the magnificent coda spoken by both ALP and the river. On the hypothesis that the *Wake* is the continuous product of a dreamer, this coda implies either that there are many dreams (and, perhaps, many dreamers) or that the same dream must be dreamt by different characters—in relays, as it were.

One might dismiss these contentions as mere quibbles based on a too-literal understanding of the *Wake* as dream. I myself believe that such problems are not mere quibbles, but rather indicate that we must make interpretive distinctions before the dream aspect of the *Wake*'s structure can be properly situated. Now, in general, we may describe the language of the *Wake* as dream language. But it is essential to locate what might be called the referential status of this dream language as precisely as possible. We must distinguish between language as representative of the actual process of dreaming and language incorporating aspects of the process of dreaming as applied to dimensions of reality transcending the limits of sleep. In short, dream language need not necessarily be about just the process of dreaming; it may also be about something other than that process. The assumption that dream language can, perhaps even must, refer only to dreams and nothing else reduces the referential scope of that language. But surely dream language can be applied to something other than the psychological process within which it first occurred.

In fact, this kind of language may be appropriate for illustrating a certain metaphysical vision of reality, not merely the reality which, in dreams, appears to be in some respects alien to waking reality. Thus the word "riverrun" may be viewed simply as a linguistic collage representing the floating dreamy experience of a body of moving water. But from a perspective somewhat removed from the immediacy of a dream, it may also connote the possibility that we must reconsider a common metaphysical distinction, that between an entity and one of its essential properties, precisely because of that very intimacy. To assert the presence of the metaphysical perspective is not to deny the presence of the dream; it is, however, to extend the dimensions of dream language beyond the limits of dreaming as a particular type of consciousness in order to interpret the significance of that language within the expansive confines of the *Wake*'s world.

This distinction allows us to answer the three problematic aspects of the dream hypothesis. The first two characteristics of the *Wake* described above, the shifts between straight prose and puns, and between dream language and waking language, may be considered mutually compatible. If dream language and the prevalence of puns are somehow essentially related, then the straight prose which appears periodically in the *Wake* would, from the metaphysical perspective suggested above, become language not necessarily of waking consciousness, but language reflecting a traditional literary representation of the extralinguistic world. We are thus not compelled to explain away the marked stylistic differences within the *Wake* as we would have to do if we accepted the premise that the entire *Wake* gives the illusion of replicating a dream. The speaker of dreamlike language need not be understood to be dreaming, although it may well happen that in the process of narration he (or she) becomes assimilated within what is being narrated, that is, presented as becoming absorbed in the content of the dream as that content is being related. But the narrator nonetheless remains to some degree apart from the purely psychological limits of the dream. It is as if one were always simultaneously awake and asleep.

And as for the final characteristic, the *Wake* may in fact be narrated by many distinct individuals. The language each narrator employs may be of the same dreamlike sort, but since we have seen that the mere presence of dreamlike language need not imply that the narrator is dreaming, there is no problem in having a number of different characters speaking dream language, just as there is no problem in having a number of different people speaking Irish or English. There is a problem, however, if one restricts dream language to that of the psyche of a *single* dreamer, whether it be James Joyce or someone else.

(2) What are the principal implications of this interpretation of the *Wake*'s language? I have argued that the language of the *Wake* should be located both inside and outside the world of dreams. The fact that the *Wake* as a whole has been thus situated implies that the reader should approach its narrative as a

complex interplay of two apparently different yet related perspectives on reality. The problem then becomes as follows: does the *Wake*'s dream language represent a recognizable structure? If so, to what extent is that structure metaphysical? And if it is metaphysical, is the content of that metaphysics basically identical with, only tangential to, or dramatically different from, the metaphysics of waking reality? We can answer these questions only after carefully studying the *Wake*. However, these questions cannot be rejected as irrelevant simply because of the dreamlike character of the *Wake*'s language.

Even those who insist that the entire *Wake* is a literary recreation of a dream should keep all of the above considerations in mind. Dream language may appear to be gibberish (Burgess's word), but it does not follow that gibberish is without an underlying metaphysical structure. Such gibberish may well reveal a purpose and a message to an attentive audience. The more we know about this structure, the more we know about the relevance of the *Wake*'s language to waking consciousness. One might expect that the world defined by the *Wake*'s dream and the world of waking reality have little to do with one another. However, should we discover that the metaphysical structures of each domain share common elements, then what is true of the world of the dream may also be true of the waking world, regardless of who in or out of the *Wake* is doing the dreaming. Furthermore, this metaphysical vision may possibly illuminate hitherto hidden regions of both the dream world and waking life. On this supposition, *Finnegans Wake* would become as worthy of close philosophical study as of literary study.

Metaphysics and the Language of Humor

The studied seriousness of philosophical discourse is ostensibly far from the irreverent gaiety of humorous language. Joyce himself said of the *Wake*, "It's meant to make you laugh." How then can the *Wake*'s humor be interpreted as possessing philosophical seriousness? Any answer to this question must consider why philosophical discourse is serious.

Consider the patently metaphysical proposition "everything is in flux." Why is this assertion philosophical? First of all, note that whether or not it is philosophical does not depend on the demonstration of the proposition's truth or falsity. Thus "everything is in flux" would be true for Heraclitus whereas it would be false for Plato; in either case, however, the proposition remains philosophical quite apart from its truth-value. Although it may appear somewhat paradoxical, a false philosophical proposition may be no less philosophical than a true philosophical proposition. We must therefore distinguish between the content and manner of expressing a proposition on the one hand, and the truth or falsity of that proposition on the other. Something about the *content* of the proposition elevates it onto the philosophical plane regardless of whether or not it is true.

Perhaps the distinguishing characteristic originates with our emotive reaction or attitude toward the content of a potentially philosophical proposition. Thus the fact that all things are in flux may, depending on circumstances, be a source of dire pain or an occasion of orgasmic pleasure. And the intensity of these feelings may persuade us that if this intensity can be traced to the proposition "everything is in flux," then such a claim must be awarded philosophical legitimacy. In fact, however, the range of possible reactions to this proposition also includes the complete lack of any reaction whatsoever. After all, many individuals neither know nor care about statements such as "everything is in flux." But surely "everything is in flux" remains philosophical nevertheless. Hence there is no reason to think that *any* kind of emotional reaction can justify calling a proposition philosophical. In short, only an accidental connection obtains between a proposition and an emotional reaction to it.

If neither a proposition's truth value nor our emotional reaction to the proposition generates its philosophical character, what does? I suggest that a properly philosophical proposition exhibits a type of universality which is independent of considerations of truth or falsity and our attitudes toward the content of the proposition. Thus a philosophical proposition is intended to reveal something universal about a given state of affairs. For example, "everything is in flux" attributes a certain condition to every existing thing, an attribution which is abstract and unabashedly metaphysical. The particular condition or property is irrelevant; the essential point is that this condition be predicated universally. Thus much contemporary philosophy, especially of the academic analytic variety, no longer feels comfortable with such sweeping and speculative claims as "everything is in flux." But even a much more restricted assertion, such as "meaning is use" (from the domain of ordinary language philosophy) is intended to be universally applicable to one aspect of that activity toward which this mode of philosophical scrutiny has been directed. The scope of philosophical universality will vary according to the style of philosophizing (since where to draw the limits of philosophical discourse is itself a philosophical consideration). The relevant point is not the degree of abstractness of the proposition or the extent of its universality, but simply the fact of universality over a given domain of reference.

For a proposition to be philosophical, it must have universal application to a certain range of referential reality, ultimately, of course, to determine the truth about that aspect of totality. Now if determining philosophical truth is a serious business, then propositions purporting to disclose philosophical truth must themselves be taken seriously because they represent this seriousness linguistically. Such seriousness may link the language of philosophy with literary language animated by philosophical considerations.

Critics frequently assess literary works from a philosophical perspective; they do so when they speak, more or less covertly, of the "truth" present in a particular literary work. Surely, to speak of truth, however loosely defined or understood, is to speak of what has traditionally belonged to philosophy. Of course, this in no way excludes truth from literature—Plato's quarrel between poetry and philosophy, a quarrel already ancient when he mentioned it in the *Republic,* may well never be resolved. The point is that philosophy aims at uncovering some sort of truth, whereas literature may or may not pursue this end. Furthermore, making philosophical propositions in pursuit of truth is an activity regulated by certain rules of form (for example, coherence, consistency, and universality). And it seems fair to say that philosophy has been more attentive to these factors than has literature, especially in its concern to elucidate the relation between formal logic and informal language.

That some works of literature succeed in expressing truth shall not be questioned here. But if literature does admit of truth, then will one type of literature be more "true" than another? The answer is no, at least in terms of the theoretical standpoint argued above. There is no reason why a suitably philosophical proposition cannot be derived from any type of literary language. The only relevant prerequisite is that the work in question be construed so that appropriately universal propositions can be elicited from its structure. It has been argued that the language of drama, particularly tragedy, customarily strikes us as "more philosophical" than the language of humor. However, this argument is unpersuasive; one may experience the *Wake* as both humorous and metaphysically grounded.

The language of tragedy clearly impresses us as serious, but the seriousness of tragedy is not equivalent in all essential respects with the seriousness of philosophical discourse. Philosophy is serious in seeking true propositions which are universal, whether the scope of that universality includes the totality of human experience or all phases of one aspect of experience—the moral, the aesthetic, a certain language game, etc. Tragedy is serious because it presents conflicts in which individuals must resolve problems. Thus the seriousness of "everything is in flux" is not indentical to, say, the seriousness of Oedipus struggling with an apparently disordered universe whose laws are strangely hidden. After all, the seriousness of Oedipus' situation may never pertain to any other individual. An element of that situation (or, in general, any situation in any drama) can, of course, be transformed into a properly philosophical proposition—"every human action is determined by destiny." But this assertion pertains to a universality—all human affairs—which manifestly outstrips whatever may happen to that individual who is Oedipus.

Now if the situational seriousness of tragedy differs generically from the seriousness of philosophy, then surely we may infer that the situational levity of comic literature need not preclude the possibility that comedy can also have philosophical significance, although the seriousness of philosophy achieves its reality on an altogether different level. In other words, there is no reason to think of tragedy as a literary form of more intrinsic philosophical character than comedy, or any literary form in which humor plays an essential role. Therefore, as long as the requisite universality can be obtained, it is just as possible to elicit a philosophical relevant proposition from literary humor as from literary tragedy. It would doubtless be mistaken to assume that all humorous writing is secretly sodden with philosophical subtleties. My point is only that it would be just as mistaken to assume that humorous writing is necessarily devoid of philosophical significance simply by virtue of the various forms of laughter which that kind of writing tends to evoke.

Some may still balk at this particular approach to the *Wake*. Those who believe at some level of consciousness that life partakes more of the darkly tragic than of the luminously comic will regard humorous writing as a respite, perhaps even escape, from the shadowy run of life's workaday events. Such people are not inclined to penetrate the protective buffer of humor for purposes of scrutinizing the metaphysics which may lay hidden within its comic texture. This disinclination assumes prominence because the experience of humor generated by this type of writing would for some readers lose its inviolate and protective character once that experience became subject to reflective analysis. However, must it follow that comedy will lose its capacity for exciting laughter and release once it has been subjected to an inquiry which approximates philosophical criticism? In some instances, possibly—but surely not when the work under analysis is *Finnegans Wake*. I take it as axiomatic that the *Wake*'s limitless complexity will overwhelm any attempt to unravel its structure, however sustained or rigorous. The intimate juxtaposition of such apparently disparate perspectives on the world merely provides further testimony to the universality of Joyce's literary genius.

PART I
In the Wake *of Metaphysics*

The Reality of Flux

One of the most frequently quoted phrases in *Finnegans Wake* is "the book of Doublends Jined," a locution which contains, among other things, perhaps the first explicit mention of the *Wake*'s circular structure. Here Joyce intimates that once the reader joins the double ends of the sentence which "begins" on the last page and "ends" on the first, the *Wake* will start repeating itself, thus becoming a work without beginning and without end. However, the sentence in which this phrase appears is equally important. It reads:

> So you need hardly spell me how every word will be bound over to carry three score and ten toptypsical readings throughout the book of Doublends Jined (may his forehead be darkened with mud who would sunder!) till Daleth, mahomahouma, who oped it closeth thereof the. Dor. (20.13–18)

Here we are notified that "every word" in the *Wake* will have multiple readings, in fact, the same number of readings as the biblical life span of the ideal reader who devotes his life to the *Wake*—threescore and ten. What verges on an Old Testament curse enjoins us to accept the fact that every word (not just the puns) will stand for an indefinitely large number of meanings.

Assuming that the threatened mud of this curse will move us to seek a lifetime's worth of meaning in the *Wake,* only death itself closes the door on the subsequent search. *Finnegans Wake* will then become our wake as well.

All conventional semantic limits of language have thus been virtually eliminated in the *Wake.* Each linguistic element will concurrently convey many meanings and point to many possible referents. From the standpoint of literary style, this internal complexity establishes a seemingly endless horizon of literary significance. And from the standpoint of metaphysics, this concurrence of untold meanings and referents all within one word testifies to the fact that a condition of flux has been established between the surface significance of the word or phrase and the meanings and referents incorporated within each such linguistic component. Once this condition of flux has been set into play, any attempt to stabilize the flux at a point somewhere short of its proper dimensions (if, indeed, the notion of "dimension" can be applied in this context) risks distorting the full meaning of each word in the *Wake*'s fluid prose.

This prescriptive warning about the limitless semantic and denotative range of the *Wake*'s language should be taken seriously. It will compel us to strain our literary sensibilities and intelligence to the utmost in order to discern nuances and connections which may not be visible when the text is read as literature is usually read. Why should we undertake an exercise apparently fated to fall short of anything like completion if our knowledge remains less extensive than that of the *Wake*'s author? This question is answered in the course of the *Wake* and the answer concerns the very nature of reality itself. For the prescriptive declamation announcing the *Wake*'s semantic fluidity receives a full-fledged, if intermittently expressed, metaphysically descriptive underpinning. The language of the *Wake* assumes its unique form because that language has been integrated within a metaphysical structure in which the forms of reality as we commonly experience them no longer apply. Language becomes out of joint with our present sense of reality precisely to mirror the out-of-joint condition of reality itself. It is an especially profound index of the *Wake*'s genius that its concern for evoking totality includes a statement of the abstract conditions which must be met before that totality can assume the stylistic form that it displays.

How shall we begin to substantiate this assertion? One pair of metaphysical concepts crucial to this type of analysis is motion and rest. However, to stipulate a definite point of departure when the inquiry intends to deal with metaphysical fundamentals is to risk the charge of arbitrariness. After all, one could argue that some other concept or pair of concepts is as crucial as motion and rest, if not more so. As we shall see, textual reasons can provide good grounds for this selection, but in any case motion and rest will be complemented by three other notions of commensurate generality—identity and difference, space and time, cause and effect. A comprehensive exploration of the *Wake* using these four pairs of concepts will indicate how the distinctive totality of the *Wake*'s linguistic world has been made accessible through metaphysical determination.

Each of the four pairs of concepts establishes its own special place as a metaphysical guidepost and also blends with the others so that their collective presence can be felt throughout the *Wake*. To appreciate the absolute pervasiveness of these principles, we must set our metaphysical ear at the highest possible pitch. Each sentence in the *Wake* must be read as if it were a potential metaphysical microcosm unto itself. Some sentences, especially long and complex ones, will provide examples of the full panorama of the notions to be sketched below. But once every sentence, regardless of length and complexity, assumes its role in the four parts of the *Wake*, the comprehensiveness of the *Wake*'s metaphysical vision will become undeniable.

Motion and Rest

Perhaps the most straightforward statement of a metaphysical principle with manifest universal scope occurs in the professorial preface to ALP's "mamafesta." There we read that "every person, place and thing in the chaosmos of Alle anyway connected with the gobblydumped turkery was moving and changing every part of the time" (118.21–23). In a word, all is flux. To the extent that persons, places and things exist as distinct entities, they collectively constitute the cosmos; but to the extent that every person, place and thing is changing "every part of the time," all is chaos. The result is cosmos-chaos. Or, in another word, "chaosmos." But surely our foreheads are about to be spattered with *Wake*-thrown mud, for such relatively nice linguistic analysis seems to violate the canon just laid down, that is, that under no circumstances should any word be sundered in order to yield comfortably recognizable meanings in the way that words tend to be comfortably meaningful. If, here and elsewhere, where such exegetically derived meanings are not available, then "chaosmos" compels the reader to experience a world in which ordered stability and disordered flux are somehow merged so that they become virtually identical. And this metaphysical consequence can be made even more precise: for each being in the *Wake* made stylistically determinate as a being of this or that sort with this or that identity, there is "a being again in becomings again" (491.23), with the number and form of becomings apparently limitless for all such beings. If everything is always in flux, then in the fullness of time each being can become, at least theoretically, any and every other being. The *Wake* is a model of consistency, intoning, "In the becoming was the weared," (487.20); the world wheels about in a becoming which is always beginning.

To deny stability by endorsing continual movement commits one to certain rather stark metaphysical consequences, and some of the more prominent implications of this principle will be examined in part III. For now, we may note the fact that the language of the *Wake* not only accepts these consequences, it celebrates them with a unique blend of energy and joy. If, for example, everything is continually in motion, then what is said of one thing can and perhaps eventually must be said of all things—"It is the same told of all" (18.19–20), or, again in a word, "Itiswhatis" (223.27). What must be told? That "everything's going on the same or so it appeals to all of us" (26.25). This particular metaphysical premise suggests that what appeals to all of us is nothing other than what appears to all of us, that is, "the allimmanence of that which Itself is Itself Alone" (394.32–33). "Itself" has become capitalized because the word now oscillates between its indeterminate referential universality as a pronoun and its status as a metaphysical proper noun (akin, perhaps, to Hegel's Absolute) representing the fact that everything individual merely participates in one all-comprehensive "It." The immanence conveyed by the reflexive character of the pronoun thus pertains both to each thing as part of the whole and to the whole itself.

But even if the whole is the same as itself insofar as it is continual motion, what about those aspects of the whole commonly experienced as parts which have seemingly come to rest? Let us eavesdrop on Muta and Juva in conversation. Muta asks:

> So that when we shall have acquired unification we shall pass on to diversity and when we shall have passed on to diversity we shall have acquired the instinct of combat and when we shall have acquired the instinct of combat we shall pass back to the spirit of appeasement? (610.23–27)

Juva acknowledges with approval the rightness of this hypothesis (as would HCE and ALP, Shem and Shaun, the two washerwomen, the four evangelists, and presumably every other set of characters if they were disposed to indulge in speculation on their own metaphysical identity). A slightly sundered restatement of this remarkable claim would include the fact that the one must become many, that the movement to multiplicity inspires a spirit of hostility, and that quelling this hostility reduces multiplicity back again to the quietude of unity. In other words, the many comes from the one, but the many continually wars within itself in order to return to the one. Yet since there always are or at least appear to be pluralities, there will always be varying degrees of tension between unity and diversity, and ultimately between motion and rest.

This tension becomes so universal in scope that it affects the very form of the *Wake* as well as what is said within the *Wake.* Notice that, strictly speaking, what the reader first confronts in the work is not "riverrun," but (on the preceding page) the single Roman numeral I, indicating the first of four parts. Presumably the fact that the *Wake* has four parts is not an entirely arbitrary formal device. But if the metaphysical principles enunciated *in* the *Wake* are also about the *Wake* itself, then this division of a moving unity into four apparently stable parts must be taken as but a provisional attempt to order what cannot be ordered. And, in fact, this implication applies not only to the fourfold partition of the *Wake* as a narrative whole, but to each of the episodes in each of the parts. What appears to be about a given person, place, or thing can never really be so specified. All narrative differentiation rests on whatever surface meaning seems to resonate most predominantly throughout the context of each episode. Thus any aspect of the narrative the reader has induced to come to rest for purposes of winning an understanding of it must necessarily be set into new and different semantic motion in compliance with the most fundamental tenet of the *Wake*'s metaphysical structure.

Identity and Difference

The *Wake*'s form seems to dissolve before our very eyes, assuming of course that the metaphysics of the *Wake*'s content applies to the *Wake* itself as an entity affected by that content. This peculiar self-reflexivity epitomizes the extent to which the *Wake* attacks apparently solid and sacrosanct metaphysical principles. The fundamental presence of a one at rest (for example, the *Wake* itself) in continuous tension with the many in motion (for example, all possible meanings of the *Wake*) permeates all other subsequent distinctions and concepts purporting to differentiate a formless flux into recognizable shapes and individuals. Consider, for example, that distinction between an entity being the same as itself and irreducibly different from its opposite. Surely no metaphysical principle is more self-evident. And yet the *Wake* does not agree. Thus, the "equals of opposites, evolved by a onesame power of nature or of spirit" are nonetheless "polarized for reunion by the symphysis of their antipathies" (92.9, 11–12). Opposites, whether subjectively conceived or putatively objective realities, spring from that one and the same power of nature by which all things flow. As a result, opposites become synthesized and fused with nature ("symphysis"), the flowing womb of all, however antithetical and polarized these opposites may be with respect to one another.

The same point may be educed from this delightfully penetrating passage, somersaulting with reversed Latin pronouns and phrases and plays on the name of the philosopher Bruno:

> When himupon Nola Bruno monopolises his egobruno most unwillingly seses by the mortal powers alionola equal and opposite brunoipso, *id est,* eternally provoking alio opposite equally as provoked as Bruno at being eternally opposed by Nola.
>
> (488.7–11)

The conflict within the individual ego of Bruno is no less intensely universal ("eternally" occurs twice in this passage) than was the warlike strife between the duo of Muta and Juva cited earlier. Apparently the author of the *Wake* sensed that keeping a flux flowing fluidly forever is no facile feat.

Identity and difference are an especially basic set of opposites, and therefore we should expect that their disappearance into an even more primal flux will not be easy. For example, the need to maintain the stability of identity is found in the description of HCE: "An imposing everybody he always indeed looked, constantly the same as and equal to himself and magnificently well worthy of any and all such universalisation" (32.19–21). But if all opposites, regardless of their metaphysical primordiality, are nullified by continually flowing into their own counterparts, then it should also come as no great surprise that the identity of HCE as well as any other distinct individual will dissolve itself into pure difference, or difference without apparent limitation. Such fragmentation occurs when HCE becomes transmogrified into myriad characters (as he is on pages 58–61) and when he is displaced geographically all over the globe (as he is on pages 552–55). The question then arises whether the phrase "the same as and equal to" can be predicated of such a multiform being. It seems that the fact of difference of this epic sort must surely swamp the claim of identity. For in what sense is it possible to assert that the many is identical to HCE if the difference between what HCE is and what he (she? it?) is not can no longer be preserved?

Nevertheless, for all its concerted emphasis on flux and the implications of flux, the *Wake* does not ignore the need to counterbalance the formless sweep. Note the parenthetical remark, uttered as if the author were speaking to himself, that "you must, how, in undivided reawlity draw the line somewhawre" (292.31–32). And again, in what appears to be a tone of self-admonition—"there is a limit to all things so this will never do" (119.8–9). And to reinforce the necessary presence of individual identity in even the most fluid of contexts—"But there's a little lady waiting and her name is A.L.P. And you'll agree. She must be she" (102.22–23). Short but rhythmic sentences and a lack of puns make it difficult to miss the relevant metaphysical point. If ALP is she, then surely HCE is he—and if she is she and he is he, then perhaps these twain will never merge to the point of losing their distinctive individuality. To conclude on a hopeful metaphysical note, "we only wish everyone was as sure of anything in this watery world" (452.29–30). But can the possibility of difference, both in the metaphysically abstract and in the concretely actual, still be maintained?

It is perhaps worth emphasizing that from the standpoint of traditional modes of thought, difference is metaphysically no less fundamental than identity. Persons, places and things differ from one another. I am not identical to my typewriter, nor is either identical to the room in which I work. But if everything is really in a condition of metaphysical flux, then at some point it will become impossible to determine precisely what differentiates that aspect of the flux which appears to be me from that aspect of the flux which appears to be my typewriter. We may speak of the difference between entity *X* and entity *Y*, but ultimately there is no ground, according to the *Wake*, for believing that any real difference between these two entities actually exists.

This implication of the flux principle receives a distinctively Joycean enunciation in the following text:

> Whence it is a slopperish matter, given the wet and low visibility (since in this scherzarade of one's thousand one nightinesses that sword of certainty which would identifide the body never falls) to idendifine the individuone. (51.3–6)

Arising from the context of the Arabian nights, dream language transforms the literary charade of Scheherazade's thousand and one nighttime tales into a metaphysical denial of the possibility of individuation. The sword of certainty, deftly eluded by these coy linguistic spells, fails to make an indentation on her body. And, by metaphysical extension, this same sword now neither identifies nor defines any one individual being so that identity can be predicated of it. That scientific sword which, upon descent, would cut off a portion of the flux so that it became a "this" rather than a "that" just hangs there suspended while everything passing beneath its sharp potentially defining edge remains essentially formless.

The phrase "idendifine the individuone" is, as it were, a particularly effective stroke. Something must be identified as *an* entity before it can be defined as a being of this or that type. The two processes, identification and definition, are normally distinguished from one another in philosophy, with identification primarily described in terms of perception and definition usually based on the adoption of a certain conceptual scheme. The *Wake* verbally merges the two processes into one undifferentiated activity, then casts doubt on the very possibility of that activity being performed on all bodies, just as it has been left unperformed on the undented body of Scheherazade.

At this point, we might stubbornly maintain that the *Wake*

seems to be gnawing away at the pen from which it took shape, not to mention at the instrument of rationality and purpose guiding that pen. For of all the many paradoxical ramifications consequent upon the principle of universal flux, that just described is surely the most quixotic and the most unsettling. But there are other effects which, although perhaps less dizzying, are equally far-reaching and important for extending the universality of the flux principle into the region of identity and difference. For example, the flux principle also makes its presence felt in terms of what might be called the infinite relativity of beings. Each entity in the world of the *Wake* "flows" into each and every other entity in the sense that the identification of *this* being also establishes a concurrent set of relations with all that is *other than* this being. Because of this peculiar omnivorousness, each apparently distinct referent in the *Wake* readily yields itself to something other than itself, with language merely serving as the external manifestation of this process of dissolution rather than its sole underlying source.

Consider one apparently clear-cut example of preserved difference—it seems evident that the identity of one self differs from the identity of another self. I am not James Joyce. Joyce is not Nicholas of Cusa, the twelfth-century philosopher. Or is he?

> Now let the centuple celves of my egourge as Micholas de Cusack calls them,—of all of whose I in my hereinafter of course by recourse demission me—by the coincidance of their contraries reamalgamerge in that indentity of undiscernibles.
>
> (49.33–36; 50.1)

The cell of my self includes far more than a centuple of other selves, just as the number of meanings read into each word in the *Wake* far exceeds threescore and ten. My ego urges me into becoming an "I" whose being transcends the limits of the "I" which I now believe myself to be. A male becomes a "sonhusband," a female becomes a "daughterwife" (627.1,2); indeed, all differences between the sexes are now groundless since,

Teutonically speaking, "himundher" (92.9) describes what we all are. Thus, "I is a femaline person" (251.31) follows logically from the fact that I am "manorwombanborn" (55.10), a metaphysical process occurring regardless of whether or not the individual self has even the barest inklings of such extensive self-differentiation. However contrary these multiple selves may appear, either in company with that "I" which I call myself or with any other self, they nonetheless remain "coincidancing" within whatever surface limitations pertain to this or that individual ego. This union does not simply amalgamate contraries, nor does it reamalgamate them; rather, contraries are "reamalgamerged" so that the metaphysically sensitive reader of the *Wake* becomes subject to as many self-transformations as do the central characters (character?) of the *Wake* itself. For *"Shem and Shaun,"* the *"shame that sunders em"* (526.14) has no justification, whether in the parlance of printing or in the traditional modes of metaphysics.

Universal flux has dissolved all real differences between individual beings, thereby setting into motion an unending series of fluid relations among all apparently discrete beings. This particular repercussion assumes special prominence in considering the self as one kind of being. It seems true to say that an individual self apprehends other selves as other by existing in relation to those selves. The more individual egos a given self has experienced, the more the limits of that self are extended. Now to affirm that I experience many selves other than my own ego presupposes that I can relate to all these selves in some way; however, I must retain the unique reality of my ego as distinct from these other selves in order to preserve the difference between myself and others. To the extent that a reader of the *Wake* merges with, say, HCE in the experience of reading about that character, to that extent an identity of sorts exists between these two selves. The reader *is*, in some sense, HCE (just as, in some sense, HCE *is* the reader). The same sort of identity emerges whenever two individual characters interact with one another within the metaphysical confines of the *Wake*. Yet surely no one would think of denying that however engrossed one becomes in the *Wake,* the reader and HCE remain distinct individuals of vastly different metaphysical types. And similar considerations would seem to apply within the *Wake.* But precisely to what extent do individual characters in the *Wake* remain individual in any discernible sense?

This problem concerns the fact that the limits necessary to establish the difference between selves (or between literary characters) begin to blur because of the omnipresence of the flux. Should the metaphysics of the *Wake* be extended to the point where the individuality of no character can be preserved? If so, then in effect everyone is no one, since anyone is really the same as everyone else, given that the very possibility of difference between or among them has been ruled out by implication. The apparently indeterminate limits of the flux must be settled somehow not simply for the sake of pursuing the question as having intrinsic metaphysical interest, but more importantly in order to determine the status of individual characters in the *Wake* (if, indeed, there be any). We must therefore discover, if possible, the extent to which the flux principle can admit of real differentiation. The greater the degree of differentiation, the greater the possibility for preserving the uniqueness of individual characters within the flux. After all, whenever days were nights and nights days (549.6), it would be impossible to tell the difference between being awake and being asleep, not to mention the impossibility of ever really knowing what's what.

Space and Time

A condition of universal and eternal flux implies that any apparent difference between entities can only be illusory. And the same illusion results when identity and difference are not allowed to coexist as fundamental principles of reality. The *Wake* provides additional support for this consequence by explicitly reflecting on two other metaphysical aspects of reality, space and time. One traditional way to differentiate between entities is to recognize that they exist apart from one another in space and time. However, the possibility of differentiation provided by standard notions of space and time quickly vanishes as soon as these notions themselves become subject to the maelstrom of the *Wake*.

The principal abstract characteristics of temporality can be derived from the *Wake*'s metaphorical statements. Time is depicted as a road, but a road which has no final destination point because it never really had a definite point of origin—"the Vico road goes round and round" (452.21–22); it "moves in vicous cicles yet remews the same" (134.16–17). The result, "cyclewheeling history," is marked by a "continuous present tense" (186.2,1). The meaning and implications of this kind of temporality are as intriguing as they are vertiginous.

Time as a Continuous Present

The question whether the concept of history depends on a certain experience of time or whether time itself emerges from some primordial historical sense remains a classically difficult metaphysical problem, and one which we cannot discuss here. We shall begin by assuming that time can at some point be distinguished from history. It then becomes possible to state and develop the principal properties of time as such, with the implications of these properties for the *Wake*'s distinctive sense of history following as essential corollaries.

In traditional metaphysics, time has been divided into past, present, and future, a distinction reflected (and occasionally refined) in the grammars of many languages. In the world of the *Wake,* however, time becomes a continuous present. This crucial metaphysical reduction is frequently and variously enunciated. At one level, the point is stated in pure conceptual abstractions designed to justify, or at least to indicate the reality of, the omnipresence of temporality as a continuous present. At another and more personal level, it is couched in language referring to aspects of human consciousness which are essentially connected to the temporal order.

Let us begin with abstract temporality. The remark "If there is a future in every past that is present" (496.35–36) jumbles the three standard divisions of time, but it does so in an important and metaphysically incisive way. This complex utterance might be rephrased as follows: a past which exists in the present but yet does so as past may be said to characterize anything endowed with the capacity for exemplifying the metaphysical fullness of time. In other words, from the standpoint of its existence in the present, anything with a past has a future while existing as past, for if it lacked a future as past, it could not move from the past into the present. Thus any past must imply the future to be capable of the transition from past to present.

Note that this particular interpenetration of past with future does not yet negate the past and the future as aspects of time distinct from the present. But precisely this negation is found in the assertion that "all that has been done has yet to be done" (194.10). This seemingly paradoxical dictum highlights the fundamentally undifferentiated continuum which defines the *Wake*'s unique temporal order. What has been done represents activity in the past which continues to exist into the present; what has yet to be done represents activity in the future which must begin at some moment in a present other than that present which is, so to speak, right now. But the *Wake* insists that these activities are identical. And this identity is possible only on condition that the "no longer" of the past and the "not yet" of the future both merge and become indistinguishable from one another within the present. The present becomes time in its sweep backward into the past and forward into the future, incorporating into itself the future and the past as merely nominal perspectives of a temporality which has no such distinctions—it is a continually flowing present.

This unlimited present temporality constitutes an essential characteristic of all that exists, including of course whatever may transpire within the domain of human action. Thus the hypothetical condition that "if we each could always do all we ever did" (287.33) proposes the paradoxical possibility that perhaps we may not achieve all that we do achieve—or, more accurately, all we have already achieved in a past which is always present. In fact, this conjunction of apparently disparate temporal sectors implies that "in the ersebest idiom I have done it equals I so shall do" (253.1–2). The "ersebest" is not just a Gaelic idiom; it is also "best" because it is first (the German *erst*) in ordering the temporality of human conduct by equalizing the difference between the pastness of "have done" and the futurity of "shall do." Thus to "bring about it to be brought about and it will be" (601.4) merely recapitulates what will and indeed must be the case. What is to be brought about will always be, because whatever *is* necessarily remains the same, and does so from wherever in the circle of time we are looking and from whatever perspective on totality we care to assume.

The *Wake* complements this personal venture into the relative impersonality of the metaphysics of time by offering a symmetrical account from the standpoint of human psychology. Memory, for example, seems by its very nature to be bound by and to the past. After all, how can memory be directed toward the future since the future has not yet happened? And forgetting, the negative counterpart to remembering, is similarly related to what has been done in the past. Remembering and forgetting are different in that they are types of consciousness unalterably opposed to one another, although they are the same in that they both depend on a temporal dimension which cannot be located in the present. But perhaps this apparently sturdy distinction rests on a truncated understanding of time. Toward the conclusion of the *Wake,* the following injunction is voiced:

> Begin to forget it. It will remember itself from every sides, with all gestures, in each our word. Today's truth, tomorrow's trend. Forget, remember! (614.20–22)

In the world outside the *Wake,* it is of course possible to begin to remember, that is, whenever we set our minds to recalling something from the past which is not consciously at hand. But it is hardly possible to "begin to forget," since the act of wilfully trying to forget something will surely retain before the mind what we intend to forget, thus militating against the very possibility of accomplishing this intention. And yet, any distinction between forgetting and remembering must fade away if all events are concurrent in an ever-flowing present. As the passage cited suggests, each word will contain the memory of what has been said, quite apart from whether the intended object of memory has been forgotten or has in fact attained status as a conscious memory. The concluding cry "Forget, remember!" amounts to a conjunction of activities opposed to one another in name only. The conjunction confronts apparently distinct forms of consciousness existing within the human psyche, eternally in the present, each detailing aspects of temporality necessarily flowing into one another within that present and thus effectively eliminating any difference between these kinds of consciousness.

Human memory may be compared to a beacon shedding its light on the outermost reaches of time, with human life itself reflecting this never-ending and unlimited universality. If each individual is a monadic perspective on the totality of human history seen as a process without cessation, then the death of an individual becomes little more than a flicker in the ongoing rush of humanity. In a remarkable coupling of polar opposites fusing life and death, the *Wake* asserts for Everyman that "the death he has lived through becomes the life he is to die into" (293.3–5). We live while dying in order to die through our perpetual rebirth, a repercussion which may be as fraught with pain as it is ripe with hope. In any case, the point to be emphasized here is that the *Wake* does not shrink from drawing the most dramatically paradoxical consequences from the metaphysical principles animating its world as a whole.

The Wheel of History

The continuous present explicitly enunciated in the *Wake* points to a uniquely closed historical order on which the sequence of events in the *Wake* is based. In fact, the very process of recounting history becomes an extremely quixotic enterprise, given the peculiar temporality which must ground the possibility of history. The phrase "as Taciturn pretells" (17.3) subtly evokes the real function of the historian in this strange cosmos, linking as it does the psychology of temporality with the topsy-turvy condition of time as such. The Roman historian Tacitus does not simply tell what has happened in a past long past so that it will be preserved for the present and into an endless future; rather, he pretells what has happened, in effect transposing history (necessarily of the past) into prediction (necessarily of the future). The actual Tacitus may not unfairly be described as taciturn, judging from certain of his historical accounts of Rome's darker moments. But even without this personal characteristic, Tacitus may well have become taciturn when faced with, in Hegel's chilling phrase, the "slaughter-bench of history," even the comically abridged version of history as presented in the *Wake.* But perhaps the reason Tacitus is taciturn results from the fact that the very attempt to write history within the world of the *Wake* becomes an activity which feeds almost cancerously on its own possibility, inevitably destroying the equanimity of anyone who essays that activity. We may now attempt to indicate in more detail the distinctively self-destructive character of history as it appears in the *Wake.*

Most descriptions of *Wake* history emphasize its temporal circularity, that is, the sameness of events recurring again and again, just as the Vico road continues going round and round. This consequence is of course obvious, especially since the letter of the *Wake*'s text insists on the point more than once. But other consequences also follow, though perhaps not quite so obvious and yet equally pervasive and crucial.

In general, the concept of history depends for its formal possibility on the concept of the past: events are understood to happen in such a way as to be located in the past in relation to events which appear to happen in the present. But if time is nothing but a continuous present, then there can be no relations of "before" and "after" because there can be no past and future grounding the possibility of these distinctively temporal relations. These relations thus become derivative; they depend for their at best marginal existence on the possibility of isolating discrete events from the *Wake* as a narrative whole and then juxtaposing these events in order to establish some kind of distinction between what happened "then" as opposed to what is happening "now."

If, however, all events in the *Wake* happen in a continuous present, then all events are temporally indistinguishable. Although it is obvious that different events do occur in the *Wake,* whatever differentiates these events from one another cannot be based on time. In the *Wake,* there is no time like the present —as a result, all events must always be happening all the time. It may be objected that the principle of temporality as a continuous present, taken to these extreme conclusions, conflicts with the sequential order of the *Wake,* an apparent process of development spreading out through time. But of course it would be a mistake to confuse the time required to read about the events described in the *Wake* with time as represented in these events themselves. Although the events recounted in the *Wake* are discrete and complex, they are all related to one another like arcs on a circle, that is, as constituent factors of a whole which shapes each and every part according to the prescribed nature of the whole—circularity. History is then rightfully pictured as "cyclewheeling"; its circumference has dimension of a sort, but it can never change and it must continually wheel itself around as a circle would if circles were somehow capable of motion. Thus the temporal differentiation that seems to mark the complexity of events occurring in the *Wake*'s narrative disappears once these events are located in their proper holistic context, just as the time required to trace the outline of a circle is independent of and irrelevant to the circle as a fixed geometrical figure.

The sequential order of events in the *Wake* is like history in that the events introduced are finite in number; however, unlike any historical account (or, indeed, any work of fiction with a plot of sequential and temporal order), the *Wake* is not bound by a temporality of limited duration. The *Wake* does not, of course, explicitly mention all historical events, whether actual or possible. It contains the events which it contains, no more and certainly no less. But this is not a mere tautology, assuming that additional consequences of the *Wake*'s circular temporality are taken into account.

Let us use the term "cycle" to designate the events occurring in the *Wake,* taken collectively as a unified whole. Identity will then apply not only to each event as an individual unit, but also to the entire sequence of events. Wherever one happens to enter this sequence, the continuation of that sequence will remain the same until the entire sequence has been circumnavigated. Thus, not only do the same events recur, but also they follow precisely the same order. Furthermore, since this sequence is circular in structure, it repeats itself an unlimited number of times.

The cyclical character of historical time endlessly repeating itself displays several important, intriguing, and occasionally double-edged properties:

(1) From the standpoint of the reader traveling through the *Wake*'s depiction of history, the first cycle will doubtless seem different from the second cycle, the second different from the third, and so forth, because the reader will discern more from that history each time around. But the possibility of drawing this type of distinction between cycles of an endlessly repeating circle depends on the literary and intellectual capacity of the individual reader and remains independent of the events constituting the cycle itself. The scope of the reader's appreciation will expand, but the circular structure of what the reader experiences remains the same. And each cycle must remain precisely the same as every other cycle, for each contains precisely the same ordered sequence of words. Any distinction between different cycles must therefore be based on extratextual considerations.

(2) The *Wake*'s doctrine of a continuous present in tandem with a cyclical configuration of history forms a consistent metaphysical whole. The circular character of history allows the *Wake* to recount a vast number of episodes, all occurring as it were on the circumference of a circle with considerable—but limited—area. But since history is indeed circular, the time that can be said to transpire within the limits of history can be noth-

ing other than a continuous present, given that the circular motion of history never really goes anywhere. It has no beginning and no end, just as the present has no beginning and no end. Both the limits of a circle and the limits of a continuous present are always present at every given instant. In fact, history viewed as circular in the rigorous geometrical sense of circularity will entail that the time occurring within—or around—the limits of history must be continually present.

Any event in history understood in this sense cannot be located at some point in a past no longer present. The author of the *Wake* is well aware of the fact that what has been recounted in its annals cannot be identified in the customary modern manner—"the studious omission of year number and era name from the date" marks "the one and only time when our copyist seems at least to have grasped the beauty of restraint; the lubricitous conjugation of the last with the first" (121.28–31). This remark (rendered in straight English) blends self-deprecating irony, a dash of wit, and the recognition that introducing a date would belie the metaphysical circularity essential to history as a continual—and thus nondatable—present.

(3) Even history as circular admits, or seems to admit, at least one possible mode of differentiation, that between clockwise and counterclockwise motion. This distinction becomes especially prominent in view of the fact that the *Wake*'s narrative follows a certain sequential order. The work is read from the first page to the last—not the other way around. But the question is whether this textual datum has any bearing on the relevant aspects of the metaphysics described in the *Wake*'s language. The answer, I suggest, is no.

If the *Wake* is taken as a whole, then no episode can be said to be before or after any other episode. In fact, each episode occurs both before and after any other episode. For example, in the final pages of the *Wake*, ALP undergoes a gradual metamorphosis, and the reader naturally recognizes that her condition at the beginning of this transition precedes her condition at its termination. But this termination also and at the same time—within the englobing universality of time as continuous present

—precedes the onset of this transition. This follows from the fact that the *Wake* as a whole is not simply one sequence of events (beginning as a printed text on one page and ending on another page), but is a continuing series of such sequences, each comprising the events represented by one cycle of the *Wake*'s narrative. And we have already deduced that the whole *Wake* is not just one circle, but the same circle endlessly repeated.

As a more than curious consequence, an episode which is subsequent to another episode during the first cycle will actually precede that episode during the transition from the first cycle to the second cycle. Thus the termination of ALP's transformation at the (apparent) end of the *Wake* as occurring in the first cycle precedes the onset of that transformation in the second cycle. And since every episode in the sequence of events narrated in cycle one must be repeated in cycle two, and so on, all historical relations of "before" and "after" become completely arbitrary. As the cycles are multiplied, the same event A must happen both before and after the same event B. This rather unsettling consequence might be avoided if one appealed to some sort of hermeneutical perspective, or perhaps emphasized a certain "starting point" in the circle. But these appeals are based in turn on the premise that a circle can be generated at one and only one point and that the direction of the course of the circle somehow gives it its distinctively circular character. However, neither of these premises is viable, assuming of course a parallel between the structure of the *Wake* and geometrical rigor. (This particular aspect of the *Wake*'s structure will be discussed again in part III.)

(4) Identity and difference permeate historical understanding. Identical patterns occur frequently in history—as, for example, in the rise and fall of civilizations—but each instance of a general pattern differs somewhat from every other instance of this pattern. However, history as it appears in the *Wake* will necessarily be divested of the richness of such differentiation. To make the point in a gustatory mode, "Thyme, that chef of seasoners" (236.27), adds no flavor to the menu of history. His-

tory can never become fresh because no one event nor any sequence of events can ever be anything other than itself as a recurring arc on the never-changing cycle of circular history. For even if "we are in for a sequentiality of improbable possibles" (110.15), there are limits on those improbable possibles, that is, the denotative aspect of the *Wake's* language in conjunction with the intelligence and erudition of each individual reader.

In one important respect, this kind of historical identity begets a vicious circle, since history has been reduced to an endless repetition of the same events. Now if the letter of Vico's teaching would have it that history must be understood not as one all-encompassing circle but as a series of cycles, each of which represents a sequence of events governed by the same general pattern, then the cycle loses its viciousness whenever variety is found within a given circular sequence of events. Thus an event at a given point in one sequence will somehow differ (precisely how is irrelevant for our purposes) from an event at the same given point in another sequence. For example, one civilization might end by fire, another by ice—both are thus identical in their finitude but different with respect to the manner in which their ends come about. But the *Wake* taken as a whole cannot admit even the possibility of such differentiation, for if it did then its overarching circularity would collapse and open up the possibility that something new, something apart from the circularity of an ever present now, might appear in fact and then in word.

The delicate interplay between time as a continuous present and history as an endlessly repeating cycle of episodes yields a variety of important and consequential metaphysical properties, some perhaps more apparent than others to the critical eye. These properties have dramatically altered the traditional three-phased character of time. As described above, however, their collective force remains within a purely temporal sphere, leaving the domain of space seemingly unaffected. But the *Wake*'s reduction of time into a monistic present tense cannot be neatly divorced from a similar attack on space. That such an attack is found in the *Wake,* mounted in close conjunction with the explicit elimination of temporal differentiation, can be sensed in such phrases as "at no spatial time" (358.5). Just as there is no real time in the *Wake,* at least in the usual sense of time, so also there is no special way to indicate spatial distinctions. The phrase just cited denies the reality of a differentiated space as it denies the possibility of a special time, that is, one in which not everything was happening all at once. In the introduction to his gazetteer for the *Wake,* Louis O. Mink writes: "Not only do the boundaries of Dublin expand to include the rest of the terrestrial globe and the indefinite loci of fiction and mythology, but the very dimensions of space itself become uncertainly elastic, and sometimes transform themselves into one or more dimensions of time."[1] The *Wake*'s text does not detail this repercussion with anything like the pointed treatment reserved for time. But it is nonetheless there, as will become evident in the next chapter, once we analyze certain stylistic conventions in the *Wake*'s language for their relevant spatial implications.

Cause and Effect

The twin notions of cause and effect have undergone rough treatment at the hands of modern philosophers. David Hume initiated the attack by arguing that the concept of causality was simply the result of habit ingrained in the minds of those who believed that they detected causes in the external world. And more than a few contemporary philosophers have suggested that the word "cause" has become so encrusted with meanings that it can no longer be credited with any kind of philosophical respectability. Despite such assaults, however, cause and effect remain deeply embedded in ordinary human consciousness. And they must remain just as embedded in the consciousness of philosophers when they are dealing with the everyday nonphilosophical world.

The fixed quality of causality, like time and space, also comes under critical fire in the *Wake,* although attacks depend upon the prior cogency of more fundamental metaphysical principles and notions. For example, the common-sense idea that a cause generates an effect, and thus must temporally precede that effect, receives several severe jolts. As one should expect by now, attacks on causality originate as implications from the structure of time as defined in the *Wake.* Consider the following quasi-axiomatic claim: "we have occasioning cause causing effects and affects occasionally recausing altereffects" (482.36–483.1). Now from the standpoint of traditional metaphysics, one effect can cause another effect only if an effect resulting from a prior cause becomes a cause of subsequent effect. But the *Wake* suggests here that an effect can "recause" an "altereffect," a metaphysical possibility realizable on the supposition that the notion of a causal order necessarily moving in only one direction has been thrown into question. And that is precisely what the *Wake* has done.

In the normal run of events, nothing can be both cause and effect at the same time and in the same respect. But here, as elsewhere, normality has run its course. Let us reflect on this remarkably convoluted aside: "For was not just this in effect which had just caused that the effect of that which it had caused to occur?" (92.33–34). First of all, one might object that this particular locution is a prime example for Burgess's reading of the *Wake* as, in part, high-level gibberish; consequently, such language should never be taken as anything more than a playful romp through the often bewildering logic of cause and effect. But if we examine this comment carefully, we discern that the infinitive "to occur" terminates a line of thought which virtually identifies cause with effect and effect with cause. The temporal element in this utterance is intriguing and instructive—the repeated pluperfects direct the reader to reorient the temporality of the effect so that it becomes prior to the cause, thus reversing the traditionally understood order. If, however, a cause does not precede an effect on temporal grounds, then apparently any cause can be seen as an effect and any effect can be seen as a cause. A distinction between the two concepts becomes almost impossible to establish. And if cause cannot be distinguished from effect, then all causes are effects and all effects are causes, and thus the concept of cause preceding effect has no metaphysical significance.

The dissolution of causality as a potential explanation for the universal turbulence of the *Wake* highlights the systematic disintegration of those notions which form the metaphysical backdrop for the *Wake*'s epic narrative. Let them again pass in review. The preponderance of motion over rest results in the incapacity of preserving identity over difference. With difference overwhelming identity, it then becomes impossible to conceive of time (as well as everything else) as anything other than a continually undifferentiated flow, conveniently labeled "the present" for the sake of preserving time's most manifest appearance. And without a differentiated past, present, and future within which to locate and order serially the cause/effect relation, there is no telling what may happen to whom, when, where, and why. How then is the reader of the *Wake,* existing in a non-*Wake* reality which typically makes more metaphysical sense than not, to intuit a correlation between that reality etched in stability and the riotous tumult which the *Wake* celebrates with such metaphysical meticulousness? Perhaps the very language of this topsy-turvy world presents some kind of secret haven for the reader who senses the tension between the two worlds. But on the other hand, perhaps the stylistic subtleties of the *Wake* plunge the reader even deeper into its constantly revolving metaphysical flux. The quest for some sort of stability must therefore be carried still further, now moving into the world of words themselves.

The Flux of Language

The world of *Finnegans Wake* has been definitively characterized as a flux of unceasing motion. In fact, "flux" is perhaps too pale a term—"maelstrom" may be more appropriate, since the turbulent eddies of that cosmos roil into the outermost reaches of time and space. Any attempt to localize the limits of the *Wake*'s depiction of reality by focusing on this or that character, region, or event as a fixed moment within the flux is destined to fall short of the stipulations of the *Wake*'s own metaphysics. The maelstrom plays no favorites, affecting abstract concepts as well as concrete realities; as we have seen, even the fundamental notions of identity and causality have also been engulfed within its swirl. Although normally representing stock concepts stabilizing ordinary experience, identity and causality have now been transformed into little more than ripples of permanence. However necessary conceptual limits may be for traditional metaphysics, the *Wake* threatens to dissolve these and all other limits within the flood of everything continuously becoming something other than itself.

The preceding chapter has outlined the comprehensiveness of the *Wake*'s metaphysical structure. This chapter will extend that outline, showing how the language of the *Wake* reinforces this structure by calling attention to itself in the very process of defining how the *Wake* becomes meaningful. We shall watch Joyce achieve another distinctive fusion of the abstract and the concrete, in this case a fusion of abstract reflection on various properties of language with concrete stylistic applications exemplifying the revisionist strategy of that reflection. It will be the principal aim of this chapter to broaden the metaphysical dimension of the *Wake* by threading together the ways in which the style of the *Wake*'s language has been employed in this respect.

The last chapter opened by commenting on the passage in which each word in the *Wake* was declared to possess threescore and ten meaningful readings. This passage is also crucial for the present stage of our inquiry. For, upon reflection, it may be taken as grounding the possibility of determining the metaphysical relations between two separate and, for many contemporary philosophers, very disparate realms of reality—beings themselves and discourse about beings. We may introduce these two realms into the discussion by describing them from the standpoint of the distinction between language as referential, that is, as indicating or pointing to something other than itself, and language as having meaning. Thus the word "maelstrom" has a certain meaning in linguistic contexts at the same time that it refers to a certain state of affairs existing apart from the linguistic domain.

The attempt to describe the precise relation between how a word or sentence means something and how it refers to something has generated considerable controversy. Meaning and reference are not simply interchangeable terms. However linguistic meaning may ultimately be understood, it cannot as a rule be reduced to the referential function of language. Something referred to in language is somehow fundamentally different from the meaning of the language employed in that representation. (Much of this chapter in fact assumes relevant portions of the position just outlined.)

The *Wake* cannot be said to present an abstract solution to the problematic meaning/reference relation, but it does indirectly establish an intriguing background from which to view the mediation between the two poles of the relation. For the *Wake* must be understood as maintaining that the multiplicity of meanings conveyed by every word engenders an equivalent multiplicity of referents. In short, the more meaningful a word is, the more entities that word can referentially incorporate within its realm of applicability. Furthermore, meaning in the *Wake* is of such complexity that the number of referents is apparently without limit.[1]

From the standpoint of metaphysics, this implication establishes conditions of fluidity with respect to the relation between all those entities to which language can refer and the purely semantic function of language. Thus if an entity appearing to be a thing of one sort is really in the process of becoming something else, then any word referring to that entity will nullify its underlying metaphysical status if the meaning of the word suggests that the entity is static, definite, and imperturbable. The word describing or referring to the entity should be capable of a shift in meaning no less frequently than the entity itself shifts its metaphysical appearance. These referential and semantic metamorphoses will perhaps be more jarring than smooth—hence the *Wake*'s style, "slopbang, whizzcrash, boomarattling from burst to past" (356.32–33). Joyce would seem to be attacking our conventional and unthinking use of words and our unreflective, commonsense understanding of experience. He seems to have designed the *Wake* to shock us into a new reality by driving us through a language indicative of that reality's continual whizzing and rattling. Whether that new reality will be as bearable and as meaningful as our familiar one remains to be seen.

From the perspective opened up by recognizing the distinction between meaning and reference, we can see that the metaphysics of the *Wake* breaks the bonds of the world of the *Wake* by extending its limits from within the text itself onto that hermeneutical plane where reader and text interpenetrate. At times, the language of the *Wake* is aimed at a confrontation with the reader; here Joyce speaks directly to his audience, describing what he is doing linguistically as he is doing it. On this level, he tells the reader what the *Wake* is doing to words, why it is being done, and what the reader should be looking for as a result. Here we also find compassion for the beleaguered reader, with the author of this most unconventional work wondering aloud, "where in the waste is the wisdom?" (114.20). If there is wisdom in the *Wake,* then we must first approach that wisdom by taking into account the fact that its language remains "basically English" (116.26). But if so, then that language must give at least a passing nod to the rules of English grammar. And English grammar, like the grammar of any language, derives from a certain metaphysical attitude toward the world outside of language. Although the basic conventions of English are to a considerable degree retained in the *Wake,* they are subject to alteration whenever possible in order to dislodge the hold these conventions have on our apprehension of reality as expressed and expressible through that language.

The discussion in the remainder of this chapter is deployed around the four leading metaphysical concepts considered in the last chapter—motion and rest, identity and difference, space and time, cause and effect. As noted above, however, the emphasis has now shifted from "pure" metaphysics to the frequently unorthodox ways in which the language of the *Wake* has been allowed to flow in order to develop that metaphysics.

Motion and Rest

The concepts of motion and rest make their presence felt even in the phenomenon of written language. To state the obvious, motion is required during the process of transcribing words onto some surface for the sake of preserving them; once this transformation has been concluded, the resulting language remains at rest, only to be set in motion again when a reader relives that language while reading it. Furthermore, the possibility of animating written language so that it becomes meaningful depends on the implicit acceptance of a number of conventions: we must assume a certain stability to language sufficient to enable us to construct a grammar detailing these conventions. As it does with other conventions, the *Wake* attempts to jar what has been customarily at rest into some kind of appropriately metaphysical motion.

The Arbitrariness of Spelling and Linear Writing

The spelling of English words has become uniform. But the *Wake* insists that this convention has had disturbingly stultifying effects on words as semantic vehicles; the range of meanings which words can display in context has been restricted by the simple empirical fact that a word is laid out in a conventionally unvarying way. But in the *Wake,* individual letters will be added or subtracted to given words whenever the metaphysical need arises; after all, "it is surely a lesser ignorance to write a word with every consonant too few than to add all too many" (115.1–2). There is, so to speak, a certain intellectual prudence in compressing many ordinary words into a single extraordinary one by studiously spelling that word in a metaphysically suggestive way. The reader of these freshly minted words must set aside fixed expectations engrained by years of seeing the printed word as customarily spelled. In fact, we must stoop in order to understand the inscribed metaphysics of flux. "(Stoop) if you are abcedminded, to this claybook, what curios of signs (please stoop), in this allaphbed!" (18.17–18). If causality and temporal order no longer command the realm of beings, then the order of the alphabet will remain sacrosanct only for those too "abcedminded" to stoop to the level necessary for seeing everything that has been curiously signaled in the *Wake*'s unique claybook. Thus, "by writing thithaways end to end and turning, turning and end to end hithaways writing and with lines of litters slittering up and louds of latters slettering down" (114.16–18), Joyce hopes that individual words can be set into the appropriately cosmic semantic and referential motion.

Violating the conventions of spelling, in the *Wake,* is iconoclastic but metaphysically necessary. Other fixed conventions concerning written language are also subject to alteration. Most written Western languages are transcribed on parallel horizontal lines, "along which the traced words, run, march, halt, walk, stumble at doubtful points, stumble up again in comparative safety." But these limits are merely "ruled barriers" (114.7–9) which can and, for the epic purposes of the *Wake,* must be sidestepped. We can then see, for example, how the letter E in various positions other than upright can be taken to represent much more than merely the most frequently occurring letter in the English alphabet. Also, the layout of the type at the opening of the ALP chapter (196) forms a natural visual perspective which plunges the alert reader into the slow flowing of the river Liffey while the language itself initiates a concurrent semantic treatment of the same subject.

These examples have suggestive metaphysical overtones which transcend mere stylistic ingenuity. Such variations point to the possibility that the linearity of written language, with its neat horizontal-vertical passage down verso and recto planes, constitutes a set spatial grid. And it may well be that this grid contributes to our picturing nonlinguistic space in an analogously symmetrical way. Therefore, the more we can detach ourselves from conventional linearity and its possible metaphysical implications, the more open we shall be to alternate spatial forms, especially the type of all-encompassing space which pertains to the referential function of the *Wake*'s language (on which more shortly).

The Reduction of Nouns to Verbs

Both the spelling and the linearity of writing have been set into motion. However, these conventions are a mere threshold to a much more radical interpretation of one important aspect of traditional linguistic structure. The *Wake* asserts that the "timid hearts of words" (258.2) must be strengthened in order to withstand the onslaught of reality's flux. This striking image, giving words "hearts," bestows on language a form of existence possessed only by something itself capable of self-motion. And, in fact, this metaphor contributes a new perspective on the entrenched grammatical understanding of this noun. The *Wake* tells us that "if we look at it verbally perhaps there is no true noun in active nature where every bally being—please read this mufto—is becoming in its owntown eyebals" (523.10–12). If "verbally" here means (at least in part) "in the manner of a verb," then the claim seems to be that no "true noun" can adequately reflect the metaphysical fact that a being is always going round and round ("bally") in its becoming. The noun, traditionally understood as a word which names a being or entity in some wide sense, conceals the fact that the being keeps moving into and out of itself. Thus a verbal perspective is needed on the true metaphysical being of what is named by the noun not only to restore the "active nature" of the being so named, but also to introduce the being directly into the temporal dimension over which the verb customarily has grammatical control.

Verbs are capable of differentiation by way of tense discriminations while nouns are not; if, however, nouns are considered as verbal equivalents, then nouns, their "hearts" no longer "timid," will also become subject to considerations of tense. We need not look just to verbs for the temporal signals present in language—nouns will (or at least can) convey this dimension no less revealingly. The convenient grammatical distinction between subject as doer and verb as indicator of what and when something is being done will no longer apply, since the subject's mode of existence as noun should not be construed as static and apart from all verbally denoted processes. The metaphysics of the *Wake* commands that substantives of all sorts be set into the same kinds of motion already present in verbs and that the timid hearts of nouns must undergo everything that a continual present tense makes possible. The *Wake* itself obeys this command; thus, we read "now and here me for all times" (145.21), "when he had gulfed down mmmmuch too mmmmany gourds" (171.19), "will bee all buzzy" (238.34), and "If thees lobed the sex of his head" (354.28–29). In each passage, the verb has been derived from a noun related to the general sense of the passage. But since the coined verb is properly speaking noun and not verb, it nonetheless remains at some semantic distance from the sense that would have been present had the correlate verb been preserved and written. And yet the noun-now-verb has been given life in these contexts. And, by implication, the referent of the noun becomes situated within a verbal and thus fluid setting more in keeping with what is, the *Wake* assures us, its true metaphysical character.

The Narrowness of Verbal Grammar

But even in those cases when nouns have been restructured into verbal equivalents, it does not follow that the analyses of verbs in traditional grammar will correspond to the ways of verbs in the *Wake*. The author states forthrightly, "No longer will I follow you obliquelike through the inspired form of the third person singular and the moods and hesitensies of the deponent but address myself to you, with the empirative of my vendettative, provocative and out direct" (187.28–32). The concept of "third person" assumes a grammatical difference between the narrator and the object addressed. If I write "he says," then the "I" who writes and the "he" who says are not identical. Furthermore, the third person singular presupposes another distinction between the singular "he says" and the plural "they say." But what if, at the appropriate level of generality, "he" and "they" are identical? And what if "I" and "he" (as well as "you" and "he," "he" and "she," etc.) are also ultimately the same? We have already seen the metaphysical principle demonstrated that the flux demands something tantamount to this universal identity of personality. The letter of the *Wake*'s language is accordingly compelled to circumvent, or at least to question, any grammatical distinction which implicitly rests on a denial of such identity.

What holds for the apparent differences relating to person and number also holds for verbal discriminations according to mood. In fact, mood requires additional consideration because, unlike the relatively straightforward differentiations determining person and number, mood concerns the attitudes of the speaker toward what is spoken. And these attitudes originate within the complex human mind, a swirling source of untold attitudinal possibilities. Has English grammar dealt adequately with this rich multiplicity? We can hear the answer by attending to the following: "Kind Shaun, we all requested, much as we hate to say it, but since you rose to the use of money have you not, without suggesting for an instant, millions of moods used up slanguage tun times as words as the penmarks used out in sinscript with such hesitancy by your celebrated brother—excuse me not mentioningahem?" (421.15–20).

Our grammar books tell us that the English language has three moods—indicative, imperative, subjunctive—but here we are challenged to conceive of "millions" of moods, at least while we are in contact with the attitudes of a uniquely Faustian linguistic craftsman. To illustrate a few of these possibilities, let us return for a moment to the passage cited above from page 189 of the *Wake*. If, for example, one is involved in a vendetta, then one will speak in the "vendettative" mood; if, on the other hand, one intends to rouse a suitably erotic mood, then one will speak in the provocative mood. The number of possible moods depends only on the number of possible discriminations open to language and its capacity to translate attitudes from felt experiences into words somehow representing these experiences. The result of such openness will resemble "slanguage" only if we persist in thinking of moods according to the narrow stipulations of traditional grammar. Human moods constantly undergo change, and the appropriate linguistic identification of these fluctuations is a possibility if we widen our understanding of the grammatical notion of mood enough to reflect the flux of our moods.

Identity and Difference

The last chapter defined the notions of identity and difference and applied them to beings themselves. The context now shifts from beings to discourse about beings, but the rhythm of reasoning here is congruent with the earlier discussion. Consider the following passage as an illustration: "the world, mind, is, was and will be writing its own wrunes for ever" (19.35–36). Note, first, that the world—totality—does the writing, not that part of totality which is the human spokesman for what has been written in and about the world. Furthermore, the single outright pun in this passage is rich with import, especially with respect to the metaphysics of identity and difference. "Wrunes" means "runes," with the suggestion that this form of ancient writing is, was, and will be repeating itself endlessly. All that can be said has already been said in a distant past which is forever present—any apparently literary novelty can only be a linguistic echo. But "wrunes" is also "ruins," intimating that this endless runic repetition, perhaps temporarily exhibiting form and order, is destined by the essentially chaotic flux of language and the world to crumble into continually different if not disordered heaps of words.

Although all things, linguistic and otherwise, are moving in the *Wake*'s world, there is one apparent respect in which the *Wake* remains the same throughout all this motion. And that is the language of the *Wake* itself—and its order. Joyce does not mince words in making this point:

> My unchanging Word is sacred. The word is my Wife, to exponse and expound, to vend and to velnerate, and may the curlews crown our nuptias! Till Breath us depart! Wamen. Beware would you change with my years. Be as young as your grandmother! The ring man in the rong shop but the rite words by the rote order! (167.28–33)

Author and reader are forever wedded to the word of the *Wake*, by right, by rite, by rote, by ritual, by whatever allows us to breathe in the first place.

The global character of this claim is reflected in those parts of the *Wake* which are perhaps the most striking linguistic examples of difference merged with identity—the myriad puns. Just as, we are assured, the *Wake* itself exhibits a form of self-identity as a textual whole, so too that stylistic part of the *Wake* which is the pun remains the same as itself on the level of immediate meaning while yet oscillating between (if not among) various other meanings. Since part reflects whole in this sense, analyzing the structure of the pun may yield insight into the structure of the *Wake* as a whole.

In the first sentence of the *Wake* the word "vicus" includes both the Latin *vicus,* street or village, and the proper name, Vico. One suspects that recognizing these two different allusions within one and the same word affords little more than a faint intellectual chuckle. But other puns stimulate other reactions. For example: "Heave we aside the fallacy, as punical as finikin, that it was not the king kingself but his inseparable sisters, uncontrollable nighttalkers, Skertsiraizde with Donyahzade" (32.6–8). Surely we will agree that "Skertsiraizde" is humorous in a way in which neither the example of vicus nor any other of the puns in the *Wake*'s first sentence is humorous. But why? Recalling the complex metaphysical structure reflected in a *Wake* pun allows us to detect the presence of an aspect of that structure which becomes prominent in those cases when the pun triggers a guffaw rather than a polite chuckle.

"Skertsiraizde" sounds like "Scheherazade," but this phonic resemblance is not the primary reason why this pun is funny. I suggest that the humor results from the semantic juxtaposition of different elements of reality which are incongruous when judged according to our customary (but, according to the *Wake,* shortsighted) perceptual and metaphysical habits. From the standpoint of metaphysics, the pun brings together elements with little if any determinable relation to one another under a form of homophonic likeness. As such, the pun presents a pithy exercise in identity and difference. Thus, "Scheherazade" and "skirts he raised the" denote a certain specific individual, and a state of affairs, respectively, two referents entirely distinct from one another. But this denotative difference merges into identity within the semantic confines of "skertsiraizde." However one might intend to emphasize what appears to be the primary referent, the queen Scheherazade, the residual presence of difference in the midst of identity compels the return of the exquisitely bawdy counterpart. In general, this pun —along with thousands of others in the *Wake*—illustrates the metaphysical truth that if difference presupposes identity, then identity nonetheless includes difference within it. The language of the *Wake* is a fertile proving ground for such forms of semantic interaction, pungently instantiating a subtle but essential metaphysical principle.[2]

But at this point one becomes aware of a certain metaphysical tension as these various senses of identity and difference interplay with one another in the restricted context of the individual puns taken as parts of a whole. Although abstract and not immediately evident, this tension will eventually lead into that portion of the metaphysical core of the *Wake* which becomes, properly understood, relevant to a literary assessment of the work. Consider now what the *Wake* has said about itself on page 167, cited above, and also what it has said elsewhere about everything other than itself. It is trivially true of all literary works that, once completed, they are unchanging. However, the *Wake* as "unchanging Word" distinguishes itself in this regard by announcing this fact about itself at the same time that it asserts the continual change of all things.

How is this paradoxical conjunction of identity and difference possible? At this point, we come face to face with a literary instance of an perplexing metaphysical dilemma (at least as old as Plato's *Parmenides,* in which it played an especially prominent role). For if all things are different because they are always in motion and the *Wake* itself is governed by that dictum, then the *Wake* should always be in the process of becoming different. But we have just seen the *Wake* proclaim itself to be unchanging. Thus either the *Wake* itself does not change (whereupon it follows that it is false to claim, as the *Wake* explicitly does, that all things change, since at least one thing—the *Wake*—does not), or the *Wake* itself does change (whereupon it becomes possible that what changes is the very assertion that all things are continually in motion—a possibility which, if realized, would contradict the most basic metaphysical premise grounding the *Wake* as a whole). The result is an intricate and curious state of affairs, one brought on by the letter of the *Wake*'s language and demanding resolution, if we assume that what philosophers have dubbed the paradox of self-reference is permitted to appear within a critical inquiry concerning a "literary" work.

Let us attempt to resolve the problem just raised. One way of easing this tension would be to locate a realm of reality which is in some sense impervious to the metaphysical flux. Surely one candidate is that ontological domain occupied exclusively by the principles of logic. Many philosophers have held these principles to be virtually Platonic in that they are immutably fixed at the core of rational discourse itself. For without logical rules, discourse would surge forth uncontrolled—anyone could say anything about everything without even the possibility of contravention, for there would be no conceptual or rational restrictions on which to base an appeal that such discourse was meaningless. The rarified and abstract world of logic must surely exist apart from the effects of reality defined as continual flux.

Does the *Wake* have anything to say about the principles of logic? Yes, and what is said falls right in line with everything already noted concerning the principles of metaphysics as manifestation of perpetual flux. Consider, for example, the formulation of the principle of identity as "A = A." Now any standard logic text will maintain that A = A is a logically necessary truth; it is, in fact, a tautology, true by virtue of the very meaning of its respective components and necessarily true in order to preserve the possibility of significant discourse. But according to the *Wake,* the enunciation of a logical principle as a tautology is "tootoological" (468.8) because the purely logical meaning of that principle depends, from a linguistic standpoint, on "borrowing a word and begging the question" (93.25–26). The question begged—and thus the question that must be posed again and reexamined—concerns the relation between logic and metaphysics, between how we understand the purely formal rules which guide our discourse and how we see the ultimate principles of reality itself.

In fact, the assertion that being "too too" logical about the supposedly inviolate principles of logic encompasses even the supreme logical principle—contradiction. In the last chapter we saw that the *Wake* proclaims a metaphysics of universal flux in which everything is "moving and changing every part of the time." Consistency of thought would seem to demand that whatever holds for persons, places, and things should also hold for logical principles themselves, even if they do formally structure rational discourse about persons, places, and things. We may, however, be "contradrinking" ourselves (96.3) by an overly sober acceptance of contradiction, this most sacrosanct and stable of logical principles. The *Wake* then offers an incisive if somewhat roundabout analysis showing how contradiction in one of its classical Aristotelian formulations may and perhaps should be subject to a more primordial metaphysical mode of being. Consider this remark by the professor: "I cannot now have or nothave a piece of cheeps in your pocket at the same time and with the same manners as you can nothalf or half the cheek apiece I've in mind unless Burrus and Caseous have not or not have seemaultaneously systentangled themselves, selldear to soldthere, once in the dairy days of buy and buy" (161.9–14).

As usual, much happens in this spacious sentence. If one concentrates on the purely logical aspects of the utterance, one might notice the similarity between the first half of the sentence and the following passage from Aristotle's *Metaphysics* (1005b 18–20): "The same attribute cannot at the same time and in the same respect belong and not belong to the same subject." The repetitions and parallel rhythms linking these two apparently disparate claims are due to more than happenstance. The dry abstractness of the principle of contradiction typified by Aristotle's formulation is doubtless intended to peep through the professor's pronouncement, but not merely, I suggest, as just another linguistic opportunity for punning. For the second half of this sentence, from "unless" to the end, lays down a condition which, if satisfied, would entail the virtual dissolution of the principle so cleverly aped in the first half.[3]

This condition derives its metaphysical force from the possibility that two different entities (Burrus and Caseous) could both "have or nothave" become related to one another in a certain way (sysentangled) at the same time (seemaultaneously) at a certain moment (once in the dairy days of buy and buy). The condition posits a set of circumstances dealing with temporality, in particular with a simultaneity during which incompatible properties become fused with one another. If such simultaneity were somehow possible, then the principle of contradiction—which in its Aristotelian formulation refuses to admit that time would allow such an event to occur—becomes of questionable certainty. This simultaneity may, as "seemaultaneously" suggests, only seem to be possible. But whether or not the metaphysical possibility enunciated within the professor's version of this logical principle is capable of actualization should not be the pivotal issue. The relevant point is that the range of the *Wake*'s speculation provides abstract specification for precisely the metaphysical possibility which would guarantee the absolute universality of the flux. Of course, once the principles of logic have been hurled into that flux, rationality itself will rapidly follow. But the *Wake* proceeds undaunted along its apparently extralogical way. Whoever clings to the formal correctness of identity, contradiction, or any other logical principle will simply not be in harmony with the conditions of metaphysical totality demanded by the *Wake*.

From the standpoint of traditional metaphysics, the apparent dissolution of logical principles has consequences as dire as they are diverse. For present purposes, we shall concentrate on effects directly concerned with language. Perhaps most important is the effect on truth, or more precisely, on the possibility of truth. In general, a necessary condition for saying that an utterance is true is that this same utterance could also be judged false. Thus, truth and falsity are correlative properties —both must exist in order for either to be ascribed to something said. But the principle of contradiction, the exemplar of all logical principles, establishes the formal grounds for distinguishing between an utterance which is true and one which is false. The same utterance, spoken under the same conditions, cannot be both true and false at the same time. However, if contradiction and all other logical principles no longer control discourse and are thus held in abeyance, then the same utterance can be both true and false at the same time and in the same respect. The upshot is the dissolution of truth, or at least of that conception of truth which falls under the formally defined rubric of logic.

As a result, we should hardly be surprised to find the *Wake* subtly undermining the notion of truth. It does so by insisting that the distinction between truth and nontruth can only be arbitrary, that is, based on apparent differences which lack any substance when seen from the vantage point of the flux. Thus the *Wake* speaks of the attempt to "bring the true truth to light" (96.27). But what else is truth other than "true"? This terse pleonasm suggests that perhaps truth really includes both what is true and what is other than true. The *Wake* amplifies this putative paradox as follows. We read that "the unfacts, did we possess them, are too imprecisely few to warrant our certitude" (57.16–17), which presumably means our certitude about anything and everything for which factual evidence can be put forth. But what precisely is an "unfact"? A lie? A false assertion? An unfact need be neither—it could be an assertion, any assertion, which simply is *not* applicable within a given linguistic context. Thus, "unfact" could theoretically refer to every other possible utterance which could be but is not pronounced within that context. And, obviously, the number of such "unfacts" is very large indeed.

This use of negation to mean otherness—a sentence or sentences other than that asserted explicitly as a fact—is employed elsewhere in the *Wake*. Consider, for example, this preface to the remarkable description of Shem: "Putting truth and untruth together a shot may be made at what this hybrid actually was like to look at" (169.8–10). Now regardless of what may follow in the way of description, this pairing of truth and untruth compels us to question how, in general, the difference between true and untrue language can be determined. Yet perhaps this question is irrelevant. For if Shem is *necessarily* defined not only by what is explicitly said about him as true but also by what implicitly could be said about him as untrue, then the very distinction between truth and untruth effectively vanishes and the "truth" about Shem becomes whatever can be said in language.

Such a comprehensive mode of being is not entirely inappropriate for a penman, especially one endowed with the cosmic mentality of the author of the *Wake!*

Space and Time

We have seen how time as traditionally distinguished into three discrete and irreducible sectors is collapsed into one all-encompassing present. And the metaphysics of time is intrinsically related to the temporality reflected in grammatical distinctions. Thus it is no accident that the *Wake* carefully links the fluidity of its metaphysical speculation with the fixity of grammatical concepts.

The grammatical analysis of a verb describes its function in terms of the time proper to different types of action, thus mixing implicit metaphysics with explicit grammatical distinctions. An infinitive provides access to the elements common to both metaphysics and grammar. Unlike the infinitive forms in classical Greek and Latin and various modern tongues, in English the infinitive requires two words. Whereas it was traditionally held that the two should not be separated, splitting an infinitive no longer carries with it the opprobrium that it once did. However, the *Wake* points to a much more decisive split in the infinitive. Thus we are told, "There's a split in the infinitive from to have to have been to will be" (271.21–22). Present, past, future—what could be more fundamental than this trio of verb tenses? Surely time could not be linguistically rendered without them. And yet the *Wake* tells us that in the splitting of "to have" from "to have been" and "to will be," something was split far more fundamentally than occurs in insinuating adverbs into the heart of an infinitive. The inflection of verbs disrupts the unity of time, and the extent to which grammar depends on tense differentiations is the extent to which that particular unquestioned aspect of language distorts the fundamental character of time, a distortion ultimately more devastating than the violation of traditional grammar by the split infinitive.

How does the *Wake* compensate for the grammatical disruption of time? On the principle that the grammar available to Joyce—albeit rooted in a metaphysically deficient understanding of temporality—should correspond as closely as possible to the perpetual presence of the flux, one might have expected a stylistic gambit such as couching all verbs in the present tense. However, the *Wake* exploits every recognized grammatical tense, even while claiming that an unreflective acceptance of these tenses constitutes a prime instance of metaphysical shortsightedness. A certain stylistic reminder nonetheless appears periodically, recalling the unity of what has been grammatically sundered. The device employed, simple yet evocative, consists in writing compound verbs as one word—as, for example, "hadbeen" (42.3), "wouldbe" (42.13), "shouldhavebeen" (42.19), "canbe" (48.9), "wastobe" (62.11), "wastohavebeen" (76.33).

The difference between "hadbeen" and "had been" can hardly be represented orally; when read aloud, the two locutions sound identical. Therefore, the point of writing this and other verbs as one word must be discerned visually and may then be transcribed into an appropriately metaphysical mode. The following explanation has a certain plausibility. The compression of the multiple components of these tenses into a single term effectively reduces the temporal differentiation indicated by the separate components. The resulting unity produced by these one-word reductions of verbal multiplicity contributes to the experience of temporal plurality as itself a kind of unity. The meaning of "hadbeen" unavoidably retains its grammatical tense, but the style of its presentation invites the reader to experience the verbal pastness as just one extension of time's essential unity.

The reduction of time to a continual presence is complemented by a similar reduction of space. The metaphysics of space does not emerge in the *Wake* as explicitly as that of time, but its reality is undeniable. To locate that reality, we should consider the semantic and referential structure of the *Wake*'s language, in particular the puns. Consider again the phrase "commodious vicus" from the opening sentence of the *Wake*. Once this phrase is recognized as a pun, it then becomes evident that it generates meaning in two different directions at the same time, horizontally and vertically, as it were. The horizontal meaning emerges from the place of the phrase in the sentence; the vertical meaning comes from the associations present within the phrase as pun which produces a semantic dimension over and above the meaning restricted to the phrase by its purely syntactical position. Thus, read in linear or horizontal fashion, "commodious vicus" indicates a certain spacious place. But a distinctive vertical meaning has also been generated by the pun-function of each word in the phrase. "Commodious" represents both the spatial property of a place, a Roman emperor (Commodus, 161–192 A.D.), and doubtless commode, a euphemism for chamber pot. *Vicus* is Latin for street or village and clearly is intended to evoke the philosopher Vico as well.

It should be clear then that the unique way in which *Wake* language becomes meaningful would be drastically curtailed if any one or even several of these elements were judged to encompass *the* meaning of the whole phrase. Furthermore, we must keep in mind that these two semantic perspectives, the horizontal and the vertical, are themselves in continuous motion, not simply from word to word and phrase to phrase, but also between sentence and sentence. Such motion will become extremely complex semantically. Consider the relatively straightforward phrase now under scrutiny: the vertical meaning of commodious includes Commodus and the vertical meaning of vicus includes Vico, thereby establishing at least the possibility (and, perhaps, the actuality) of a *horizontal* semantic relation between the referents Commodus and Vico. One tends to analyze the purely vertical associations engendered by the individual pun without connecting the (so-called) secondary meanings of one pun to the secondary meanings of the next pun in the horizontal dimension of the phrase or sentence. Yet the latter relations may be just as crucial to the meaning of the entire phrase as is the relation between commodious and vicus with respect to their obvious spatial nuances. The range of these semantic possibilities depends on the vertical complexity of each pun and the horizontal breadth of the phrase or sentence as a whole. Thus, even comparatively uncomplicated phrases such as "commodious vicus" soon become convoluted semantic vehicles, and extremely long sentences (as, for instance, the sentence describing HCE on pages 39–41) throw the reader into a linguistic whirlpool in which the identities of the primary referents become lost while a flood of diverse puns rushes by.

As long as this multiplicity of meaning is kept at a purely semantic level, no immediate consequences follow with respect to the metaphysics of space. However, once the semantic function has been joined to the referential dimension of the *Wake*'s language, then the repercussions become more evident. The referents of commodious, for example, exist as (a) a certain undefined region of space, (b) a particular human being who ruled over a geographically restricted space, and (c) an entity occupying a certain amount of space but presumably at no particular locale in space. This list is hardly exhaustive, but its multiplicity is sufficient to establish the relevant point. For in order to specify the space entailed by this single term's referential dimension, it would be necessary to join a determinate place (Italy) with several indeterminate places (that is, wherever "commodious" places exist and wherever there is a commode). Such expansion of space will be required for each pun, and the more multileveled the pun, the more referents and the greater the spatial extension required to incorporate its full referential capacity.

When all the puns and the complete range of their meanings are taken collectively, the corresponding referential dimension presupposes a spatial continuum in which everything is as much "here" as it is "there." Just as time appears to be differentiated into past, present, and future, but in point of metaphysical fact is a homogeneous unity of one all-englobing present, so too space, under the pressure of the referential function of pun language, must be construed as a totality of different dimensions simultaneously present. Semantic limits for any given pun will imply referential limits controlling the extent to which the whole of space must be included as a relevant metaphysical component of that pun. But if every pun is a perspective on totality (recall the "threescore and ten" readings attributed to each word in the *Wake*), then the whole of space must be understood as essential to the referential dimension of each individual pun.

The *Wake* also abolishes yet another spatial aspect of language. Although the basic language of the *Wake* is English, this language ceases to be different from other languages to the extent that these other languages become assimilated into English, or at least that English peculiar to the *Wake*. There is in effect no such thing as a "foreign" language in the *Wake*—rather, there is just language capable of containing and dissolving all apparent differences between natural languages. The integration of languages other than English within the English of the *Wake* renders the notion of a foreign language all but impossible.

A language different from one's own is considered foreign by virtue of its temporal or spatial separation from one's native tongue, sometimes both. For the literate American, Latin is foreign because it is both ancient and distant while Gaelic, although contemporary, is foreign because it is spoken in another country. If, however, the English language, which provides a shared horizon of many other languages, then those who can assimilate those other languages can be said to exist linguistically in a much broader spatio-temporal dimension than those who cannot. To state the point with bluntness typical of the *Wake*, "he would wipe alley english spooker, multaphoniaksically spuking, off the face of the erse" (178.6–7), if such a speaker insisted that the *Wake* be translated into straight, that is, metaphysically naive and provincial, English. Anyone who has mastered the language of the *Wake* lives in high measure of harmony with the cosmos, everywhere at every time all at once.

Cause and Effect

So far I have attempted to outline the comprehensiveness of the metaphysical structure animating the *Wake* as a whole. Here I will alter the pattern of symmetry followed to this point. Instead of examining the linguistic or stylistic considerations of the cause-effect relation within the context of the *Wake*'s world, I will shift the domain of discussion to the cause-effect relation arising between the metaphysics of that world and the more comfortable metaphysics usually taken for granted by the *Wake*'s reader. Even the most zealous devotee of the *Wake* must occasionally put down the work, and once removed from its flux, a reader cannot help but be impressed by the differences —marked or subtle—between the world defined by the letter of the *Wake*'s language and that other world in which the *Wake* is just one rather minor literary part.

In the *Wake,* discourse about reality and discourse about language as part of reality are complementary. As we have observed, the language of the *Wake* itself is an illustration of the reality denoted by that language. The serious reader of the *Wake* will surely be affected by both levels. In other words, that reader will initially be compelled to examine the nature of language in general and "literary" language in particular before arriving at some kind of critical conclusion about the transformation of language found in the *Wake.* But the reader will, I suggest, be drawn in another direction as well. Once we have fully appreciated the connection between language and reality, our attitude toward reality must undergo similar self-scrutiny. It is a fundamental characteristic of the *Wake* to merge language about reality with reality itself; therefore, an inquiry into the former will entail a related inquiry into the latter. The cause-effect relation at this primordial level is virtually symmetrical. If reality causes us to speak and write about it in certain ways, then spoken and written language are themselves no less causal in directing our utterances concerning what reality "is" and what it "is not."

However, we must recall that the *Wake* is not a vehicle of systematic metaphysics, but is rather a literary work directed, at least in part, by a tersely stated and consistently applied metaphysical vision. Although it is theoretically possible to subject that vision to the same kind of rigorous analysis accorded to all philosophical attempts at describing the structure of reality, one might object that such treatment becomes inappropriate if the metaphysics in question lies embedded in what is a primarily literary work. And yet the neat distinction between philosophy and literature begins to blur before the comprehensiveness of the *Wake*. For the *Wake* virtually forces us to suspend our sense of the real, indeed, to replace it with something very different as a necessary condition for understanding it as a whole. In consequence, ignoring a critical appraisal of the *Wake*'s metaphysics becomes a potential source of misinterpretation even if one's interest in the *Wake* is solely literary. Purely literary assessment of the *Wake* is based on aspects of the work which are in some sense derivative. In terms of the metaphysics of the piece, these aspects are but effects ultimately caused by a more abstract yet essential feature of the *Wake*'s overall depiction of reality.

It thus becomes essential to explore the *Wake*'s metaphysics from a philosophically critical perspective. For if the metaphysical structure of the *Wake* results in tensions when we confront it with less unorthodox accounts of reality, then the statement of these tensions may provide clues for assessing the *Wake* from the standpoint of traditional literary criticism.

Following the *Wake*'s own hint, we have attempted here in part I to explore the sense in which the "light of philophosy" might contribute an essential insight into the labyrinthine reaches of the *Wake*. So far, a certain amount of light has been shed on both the underlying metaphysics of the *Wake* taken in the abstract and the ramifications of that abstract structure within the textures of the *Wake*'s language. The extent to which the ensuring clarity touches the literary core of the *Wake* will be matter pursued in some detail later. But for now, it is relevant to wonder whether the metaphysical dimension so prominent in the *Wake* can also be found in Joyce's earlier works. If it cannot, then we may feel confident that the *Wake* stands apart from its predecessors, at least in this one important respect; if, however, that dimension does appear in the earlier works, then we should give it some attention. For by comparing early metaphysical Joyce with later metaphysical Joyce, we will widen our appreciation of similarities and differences along the full gamut of the Joycean continuum and better understand how the metaphysics of the *Wake* functions within its place on that continuum.

PART II
Anticipations of the Flux

A Portrait of the Artist as a Young Man: The Forging of the Flux

A consideration of Joyce's earlier major works along the lines we have been following is valuable at this point not merely to place his earlier fiction in the continuum of Joyce's metaphysical thought, but also to refute charges of isolation and irrelevance in Joyce's work. Typical of this kind of charge is this comment by Francis Russell in *Three Studies in 20th Century Obscurity*: "Joyce maintained that he could do anything he wanted with language, forgetting in his logomathic isolation that language is at best a faulty tool, a poor substitute for life itself."[1] Whether or not this charge is justified (and it may be), this type of judgment is significant because it helps to establish a common background against which one can see that the openly metaphysical concerns of *Finnegans Wake* have been prepared for by the potential metaphysics of Joyce's earlier major fiction.

Russell's criticism, and all criticisms of this type, would doubtless be directed more at the *Wake* than at either *A Portrait of the Artist as a Young Man* or even *Ulysses*. If, however, the grand continuum of Joyce's work includes both his two earlier long prose endeavors, then it follows that the first stirrings of the supposed linguistic eccentricities that spurred Russell's charge may already be present in these works. Therefore, even if Russell's claim is aimed primarily at the *Wake*, the critical soundness of his assessment will depend to some degree on a metaphysical dimension common to all three of Joyce's major prose works. And on the general assumption that Joycean prose can indeed be subjected to the charge of "logomathia" or some related form of linguistic excess, surely it is reasonable to view Joyce's earlier work in light of the later to determine the extent to which style or content (or both) initiated those literary practices culminating in the sweeping metaphysical grandeur of *Finnegans Wake.*

In the next two chapters, on *Portrait* and *Ulysses,* I have adopted the same set of four pivotal metaphysical concepts as discussed in part I as guideposts directing my investigation. However, since neither *Portrait* nor *Ulysses* is as explicitly metaphysical as *Finnegans Wake,* the following chapters reflect this relatively subdued yet vital element by examining these components somewhat more informally. It is perhaps worth emphasizing that the hermeneutical assumption here is not that Joyce's major prose works will form a perfectly seamless whole in all respects, nor even that what holds for a later work is true of earlier works just because all were written by the same individual. One should not pigeonhole the work of the early Joyce into compartments elicited from the work of the later Joyce. My primary purpose here is to analyze whether this quartet of fundamental concepts has affected the style and content of these earlier works, and if so, to what extent.

Significant elements in the structure of the *Wake* are common to both *Portrait* and *Ulysses.* Therefore, even if the differences between the *Wake* and Joyce's two earlier works should happen to be in many respects greater than the similarities, knowing precisely where and how these differences are to be drawn can only sharpen the boundaries of the metaphysical dimension proper to the *Wake,* and can help us determine the extent to which early and late Joyce share a common metaphysical character.

The title of this chapter, "The Forging of the Flux," is a mixed metaphor; a flux, such as a river, can hardly be forged. But this skewed figure has been chosen with intent. The first part of the phrase should recall Stephen Dedalus's famous declaration "to forge in the smithy of [his] soul" a literary representation of the "uncreated conscience" of his race. The second term, flux, is emblematic of the whirling world of the *Wake.* "Forging the flux" thus evokes the tension between the conventional stylistic structures of *Portrait* and the senses in which they anticipate the more radical reconstruction of language in Joyce's subsequent work. The forge is to *Portrait* as the flux is to the *Wake;* nevertheless, there are important instances in which the form of the latter's flowing language has already been struck in *Portrait*'s relatively static prose.[2]

An interpretive horizon along which the entire course of *Portrait* becomes visible provides the opportunity to recognize the relevant similarities and differences between the earlier novel and the *Wake.* Accordingly, our present inquiry will be ordered more by the demands of the logic of this investigation than by the narrative sequence of events in *Portrait.* We may begin by catching up with Stephen Dedalus, a young man late for his English lecture at the university. He wanders through the streets of Dublin, musing on what he had missed—"nominal definitions, essential definitions and examples or dates of birth or death, chief works, a favourable and an unfavourable criticism side by side" (178). But Stephen is learning another lesson about language from an unlikely yet revealing source. As he meanders close to the Dublin canal, he finds himself "glancing from one casual word to another on his right or left in stolid wonder that they had been so silently emptied of instantaneous sense until every mean shop legend bound his mind like the words of a spell and his soul shrivelled up, sighing with age as he walked on in a lane among heaps of dead language" (178–79).

The possibility that language can become "dead" strikes Stephen more deeply than it would most individuals because language has become for him virtually metamorphosed into a synonym for reality. In a celebrated passage earlier in the work, we learn that words which the young Stephen did not understand "he said over and over to himself till he had learned them by heart: and through them he had glimpses of the real world about him" (62). This claim reverses the intuitive understanding of the relation between language and reality: that reality is fundamental and language merely represents reality in some derivative and difficult to define secondary sense. But the point of Stephen's remark is that language must be considered as an essential part of the reason why reality is indeed real—the way we apprehend the nature of the "external" world is partially constituted by the way we talk about the "reality" of the world. Thus the more language dies, the more faded reality becomes; presumably the converse would be that reality gains in measure and vivacity as long as language seeks and obtains new life through a diversity of expression.

The above passages reveal much about the intensity of Stephen's experience of language and his perception of its relation to, or within, reality itself. But they also contain presentiments of the more abstract metaphysical concerns which will become predominant in the *Wake.* It will be useful at this point to insert a four-part schema representing the metaphysical concepts already introduced in part I. These concerns can be specified as follows:

(a) *Motion and Rest.* The language of the shop legends is now dead for Stephen; it has come to rest, incapable of engendering any kind of semantic motion.

(b) *Identity and Difference.* Common sense tells us that words are not the same as the entities to which they refer; yet when Stephen has committed new words to memory, he catches "glimpses of the real world" through these words. This important image not only denies the apparent difference between word and thing but also suggests that the true identity of a thing cannot be divorced from the appropriate words used to identify it.

(c) *Space and Time.* As Stephen wanders through space dominated by dead language, his soul shrivels, "sighing with age"; his vibrant youth becomes instantly transformed into age, as if the duration of human life depended directly on the extent to which time could be preserved in language.

(d) *Cause and Effect.* Just the mere presence of language, whether at rest as in the dead language of shop signs or in motion as media containing the real world, causes ultimate and, depending on circumstances, diametrically opposed reactions in Stephen's soul. The limits of his experience are effects instigated by mute or meaningful language.

This list highlights the implicit metaphysical dimension at this crucial juncture of Stephen's literary autobiography. However, the fact that Stephen's experience of language both living and dead has been tinged with metaphysical elements is made even clearer. His itemized account of what had transpired at the morning's English lecture included "nominal" and "essential" definitions, a favorite scholastic area of inquiry and one blatantly metaphysical, harkening back to a distinction common to various forms of medieval realism. Although Stephen does not directly express his feelings about the morning's lesson, one surmises that he is not sorry to miss yet another exercise in the difference between definition as essence and definition as mere name. Such grammatical niceties are, for Stephen, no less sterile than the dead language on the shop legends. And if this extension be granted, one then wonders whether the indictment against shop signs could also be brought against all written language. If the form of written language depends on grammatical notions derived from metaphysical distinctions based on a distorted picture of reality, then Stephen would be just as averse to embracing the available literary styles as he is to the deadness of isolated shop language. When Stephen declares in the presence of a pontificating English cleric that "[his] soul frets in the shadow of his language" (189), this claim must be understood as directed against the unavoidable darkness endemic to their common tongue. In fact, Stephen's deep-seated discontent with the static quality of his literary education suggests that not just English but all language must somehow be revivified by being set into motion outside the boundaries of grammar in particular and of metaphysical realism in general.

Does the language of *Portrait* attempt such a task? Not directly, certainly not on the global revisionist scale of the *Wake*. But there are brief indications which prefigure several of the later stylistic devices, although the means employed are neither as radical nor as frequent as those adopted in subsequent works. Once again, a metaphysical moment in the piece points the way. When still quite young, Stephen had reflected on the curious fact that one and the same God possessed different names in different languages:

> *Dieu* was the French for God and that was God's name too; and when anyone prayed to God and said *Dieu* then God knew at once that it was a French person that was praying. But though there were different names for God in all the different languages in the world and God understood what all the people who prayed said in their different languages still God remained always the same God and God's real name was God. (16)

Such meditation—a neat bit of gymnastics with identity and difference—is quite remarkable; it is no wonder that "it made him very tired to think that way" (16). We should note, however, that in the end the young Stephen concludes that God's "real name" is and remains "God," even if in French and other languages God should be called something other than "God." One might alter the linguistic configuration, but the entity referred to remains intact throughout such attempts at verbal differentiation. Furthermore, as Stephen's reflections imply, if God's real name were indeed "God," then presumably every entity would also have a "real" name, a referential vehicle impervious to any form of linguistic variation.

Although he would hardly recognize it, the young Stephen's reflections on language represent the germ of an extreme realist theory of meaning, that is, one according to which a referent has a single appropriate naming term. And yet, one such entity is described earlier in *Portrait* so as to cast doubt on the solidity of this inductive generalization. When the adolescent Stephen is wallowing in the stupors of sin and guilt because of frequent trips into Dublin's prostitute quarter, he became haunted by the very name of the city itself: "The letters of the name of Dublin lay heavily upon his mind, pushing one another surlily hither and thither with slow boorish insistence" (111). Stephen's self-awareness is defined by disgust, and this awareness, itself permeated with surliness and boorishness, becomes associated with the name of that locale in which the lowest part of his nature had been made manifest. The disjointed behavior of the letters constituting that name, their slow motion and "insistence" on retaining their identity, suggests that the name itself has a mode of existence somehow connected to the very entity which it names. This intriguing metaphysical congruence in turn presents the stylistic possibility—fully exploited in *Finnegans Wake*—that rearranging the letters might affect not only the name of the referent but perhaps also the distinctive character of the referent itself.

What in *Portrait* occurs as, so to speak, little more than a psycholinguistic twinge will become one of the primary moving forces in the *Wake*'s treatment of language. But the language of *Portrait* does manage to set things and their properties into various forms of linguistic motion. The techniques employed are less dramatic than the radical reconstruction of words through the *Wake* puns, yet in their own way they are effective and perhaps more indicative than might first appear. Consider, for example, the straightforward expedient of writing two words as one, frequently employed in *Portrait*. In some instances—such as "widewinged nose" (178), "slowflowing Liffey" (167)—the conjunction derives from the doubtless intentional assonance produced. However, closer inspection reveals that subtle metaphysical considerations are also at play.

A well-known example of this sort of linguistic configuration appears on the very first page of *Portrait:* "Once upon a time and a very good time it was there was a moocow coming down along the road and this moocow that was coming down along the road met a nicens little boy named baby tuckoo." This is an account of a father telling a bedtime story to his son and baby talk is also appropriate at the start of the story of the artist's life. But "moocow" is not mere verbal meandering. If we examine this coinage in terms of both the type of life encountered and the individual encountering it, we see that by joining what a cow does ("moo") with what a cow is ("cow"), Joyce has mixed the role of verb with noun so as to create a vivid picture of this type of being, a picture that affirms the living reality of that being. In rudimentary metaphysical terminology, "moocow" combines a property of an entity with that entity itself, linguistically reversing the usual metaphysical order of priority to emphasize the living process of hearing the mooing of the cow rather than starting from the cow as an entity—static and lacking any differentiating motion.

The word "moocow" occurs within a context that enables us to determine its literary meaning. The metaphysical significance of the word may not be so immediately apparent, but as soon as we observe that the linguistic pattern basic to "moocow" appears frequently throughout *Portrait,* we realize that such compounds represent more than stylistic innovation for its own sake. To appreciate the full import of the implicit metaphysics, consider the following examples: "nightclouds" (163), "alldevouring" (128), "bloodred" (113), "whitegrey" (50). Each of these four compounds represents a different type of metaphysical conjunction. They may be categorized in this manner: nightclouds—entity and entity; alldevouring—entity and process; bloodred—entity and property; whitegrey—property and property. These examples are not isolated moments. Table 1, representative rather than exhaustive, illustrates the extensiveness of this device in *Portrait*'s development of language.

These newly formed compounds share a common characteristic—they transform difference into a type of linguistic identity. In each instance, this identity sets in motion the implicit static quality stamped on the referent by each separate component. As a result, the referent itself becomes capable of being

Table 1

Entity/Entity	*Entity/Property*	*Property/Property*
figtree	bloodred	strangelooking
fellowcreatures	sootcoated	whitegrey
fellowsufferers	rosesoft	nocoloured
fireshovel	sandbuilt	suddenwoven
kitchengardens	turfcoloured	plumpbellied
nightclouds	hamshaped	redhot
seadusk	woodbegirt	greygreen
soupplate	hazewrapped	hornybrowed
seventyseven	salteaten	softworded
studyhall	rainladen	silentmannered
dwellingplace	silverveined	deeprooted
figseed	fireconsumed	sourflavoured
kitchengirl	bellbordered	greyblue
scullerymaid	silverpointed	brightclad
	zincroofed	gayclad
Entity/Process	gustblown	widewinged
alldevouring	twinecoloured	limphung
triplebranching	wheypale	greenwhite
slowflowing	sulphuryellow	firmfeatured
pancakeeating	fatencircled	whiterobed
trumpetblast	thoughtenchanted	onlybegotten
sunrise	rainfragrant	manycoloured
	poolmottled	
	priestridden	
	Godforsaken	
	sincorrupted	
	seaborne	

experienced according to the motion introduced semantically by the simple juxtaposition of normally distinct words here forged into a new unity. Thus, night and cloud are different, but the word "nightcloud" evokes a cloud in the night sky with an immediacy lacking in, for example, the ordinary phrase, "a cloud at night." Also, the difference between an entity as such and its constituent process, or state of becoming, begins to disappear when everything which devours is now "alldevouring." "Bloodred" links an entity with one of its essential properties, while "sandbuilt" combines an entity with a property unessential to that entity; in either case, however, the distinction between entity and property begins to blur. Finally, "whitegrey" joins different properties of the same general type —color—while "suddenwoven" fuses different properties of different types; here "whitegrey" and "suddenwoven" illustrate a common metaphysical concern to experience properties dissociated from any substantial ground as unities within the confines of a single linguistic whole.

In a work of approximately 250 pages, the fewer than a hundred individual words so styled readily merge with *Portrait*'s generally conventional prose style. Only the special context allows "moocow" to stand out noticeably, and even here the metaphysical dimension remains hidden within the immediacy of the baby-talk surroundings. But the number of such coinages is surely significant, and the subtle diversity of the various types of combinations points, if only indirectly, at an awareness of how language can control our experience of apparently discrete entities and properties in a more flowing way. This technique invites the reader to visualize difference as a kind of linguistic unity in semantic motion. What begins in *Portrait* is a seemingly stylistic idiosyncrasy, the union of diverse metaphysical elements within a single English word, can be seen as a first step toward the much more penetrating and revolutionary manipulation of language in *Finnegans Wake*.

Although not without metaphysical significance, writing two words as a unity need not be made to bear the full weight of *Portrait*'s speculation on the relation between language and reality. More full-blooded speculation on this relation exists, as we see by reflecting on passages arranged as they appear in the work. These passages deal, directly or indirectly, with individual words and how they mediate between language as meaning and language as reference. Together, the passages suggest a perspective on the relation between meaning and reference which leads to the very brink of the stylistic innovations to be pursued later by Joyce.

A. The scene is the playing field at Clongowes Wood College, and Stephen has heard Simon Moonan branded as "McGlade's suck." One might suspect that his reaction would be revulsion against the stigma represented by that term, especially in the tight confines of schoolboy society. But Stephen's sensibilities are directed elsewhere:

> Suck was a queer word . . . the sound was ugly. Once he had washed his hands in the lavatory of the Wicklow Hotel and his father pulled the stopper up by the chain after and the dirty water went down through the hole in the basin. And when it had all gone done slowly the hole in the basin had made a sound like that: suck. Only louder. (11)

Stephen has associated the word "suck" with hearing a certain sound which echoes the sound of the word. Presumably the association of experience with the sound of the word justifies his sense that the word is "ugly." The point to be noted here is the intimacy established between word and experience, even a childhood experience later grafted onto the word. For Stephen, "suck" has a peculiarly distinctive quality—ugliness—because of something that actually happened to animate his experience of that word in a certain way. It would not be surprising to discover that onomatopoetic words could be so invested with emotional or attitudinal qualities. But is it possible that *all* language has been somehow colored by such elementary forms of experience? This important point is not explored in *Portrait* except in a somewhat derivative and very personal way (see the discussion of passage D below).

B. A few pages later, Stephen reflects on one of the more captivating forms of human activity:

> What did that mean, to kiss? You put your face up like that to say goodnight and then his mother put her face down. That was to kiss. His mother put her lips on his cheek; her lips were soft

> and they wetted his cheek; and they made a tiny little noise: kiss. Why did people do that with their two faces? (15)

The "tiny little noise" represented by the word "kiss" enters Stephen's consciousness in a qualitatively different way from the sound of the word "suck" and its attendant ugliness. In fact, Stephen's concern here focuses not so much on the aesthetic quality of the word "kiss," but rather on the meaning of the action which culminates whenever the sound of the word "kiss" occurs. Furthermore, Stephen is unable to attach meaning to this sound in the way that he could to the sound produced by the inanimate rush of water down a drain. The meaning of at least this one word transcends aural associations. Sound and sense are not always consonant, it would seem.

C. Stephen relives the details of his first communion, in particular the smell of wine on the rector's breath: "The word was beautiful: wine. It made you think of dark purple because the grapes were dark purple that grew in Greece outside houses like white temples" (46–47). In this case, the beauty attributed to the word "wine" is produced differently from the ugliness evoked by the word "suck." "Wine" is beautiful, not because of its sound, but because it engenders a vision of lush colors, classic edifices, and exotic places. Visual experience has made the word "wine" beautiful, just as aural experience had made the word "suck" ugly. However, the visual experience here is purely imaginative; words representing things and places which Stephen has never personally experienced somehow become meaningful in such a way that Stephen feels confident in explaining their beauty through second-hand experiences.

D. In partial atonement for what he felt to be the brutish carnality of his sins, Stephen has entered the priesthood as a Jesuit—or so he sees himself while in a lengthy reverie. But this pious possibility fades away as the prospect of pursuing a university education becomes more than a shadowy hope. Stephen's intellectual interests are literary, but he is not certain why language has so consumed him. He draws forth "a phrase from his treasure," speaks it softly to himself, and then begins to speculate:

> —A day of dappled seaborne clouds.
>
> The phrase and the day and the scene harmonised in a chord. Words. Was it their colours? He allowed them to glow and fade, hue after hue: sunrise gold, the russet and green of apple orchards, azure of waves, the greyfringed fleece of clouds. No, it was not their colours: it was the poise and balance of the period itself. Did he then love the rhythmic rise and fall of words better than their associations of legend and colour? Or was it that, being as weak of sight as he was shy of mind, he drew less pleasure from the reflection of the glowing sensible world through the prism of a language manycoloured and richly storied than from the contemplation of an inner world of individual emotions mirrored perfectly in a lucid supple periodic prose? (166–67)

This justly famous passage has elicited much critical commentary, but no one has observed its significance for the metaphysical character of consciousness in relation to language. Stephen seeks to explain to himself why words have become so treasured. He explores several possible reasons, rejects one outright, hesitates about another, and then suggests—but does not actually affirm—that the ultimate reason depends on a relation in which "an inner world" is "mirrored perfectly" in language. No longer is Stephen's attention captured by the mystique of an individual word—now he is concerned with language on the move, with the flow of style in relation to the flux of consciousness. This shift is of some importance, and its repercussions require finer analysis.

We may begin by noting the interesting sense in which this extended reflection about prose language contains what, in the vocabulary of technical philosophy, are called self-referential elements. Thus, when Stephen wonders whether the color of words is the key factor of enchantment, he uses words which not only denote colors but also possess in themselves a certain tonal luxuriance—gold, russet, azure. And even when he suspends judgment about the "rhythmic rise and fall of words" as the crucial reason for his attraction to language, he does so in a rhythmically rising and falling sentence. Finally, the concluding sentence states the apparently decisive reason with a beautifully modulated pace, rising to a firm yet gentle crescendo, the total sentence neatly illustrating precisely the "lucid supple periodic prose" mirroring the flow of consciousness itself. Stephen has been talking about his understanding of language in language which reflects the character of that understanding. The relative elusiveness of this self-referential quality may cause some doubt concerning whether the author intended us to interpret it in this way. However, although its function is only implied, the passage clearly cuts deep into the core of Stephen's awareness of the relation between language and consciousness (and presumably Joyce's awareness as well). The self-referential character of this passage is indeed perceptible; perhaps the young Joyce had at least intimations of what more could be done by using language in this way.

However subtle, this stylistic technique in *Portrait* surely prefigures a prevalent linguistic trait of the *Wake*. But for our purposes, it will be more than sufficient to pursue the implications of Stephen's preferred explanation. For how can "inner" experience be "mirrored perfectly" in prose language, even if that language has been crafted as lucid, supple, and periodic? How can different types of consciousness be "mirrored" in this way? Stephen's claim is permeated with metaphysics, with the most obvious element being the explicit assertion that language, a medium of one type, can become closely correlated with living consciousness, a medium of an apparently different type. The truth of Stephen's avowal thus demands the existence of some sort of identity through difference. Can this identity be located and described?

Let us assume that what Stephen has stated as the most important possibility inherent in literary language has been realized, or at least approximated, in passages from *Portrait* susceptible to this sort of stylistic treatment. By carefully examining these passages, we might then be able to isolate factors for determining the sense in which the adequacy between consciousness and its literary mirror may be measured. (Even if this interpretive excursus falls short of success, the effort should help clarify the character of at least some of the metaphysical prerequisites involved in dissolving the difference between consciousness and language, one of the avowed purposes of *Finnegans Wake*.)

Here are three promising passages:

(a) As "the leprous company of his sins closed about him," the young Stephen is gripped by a grotesque fantasy populated with hideous goatish figures:

> Soft language issues from their spittleless lips as they swished in slow circles round and round the field, winding hither and thither through the weeds, dragging their long tails amid the rattling canisters. They moved in slow circles, circling closer and closer to enclose, to enclose, soft language issuing from their lips, their long swishing tails besmeared with stale shite, thrusting upwards their terrific faces. (138)

(b) Stephen approaches the confessional in order to seek absolution for his sins:

> A penitent entered where the other penitent had come out. A soft whispering noise floated in vaporous cloudlets out of the box. It was the woman: soft whispering cloudlets, soft whispering vapour, whispering and vanishing. (142)

(c) Stephen reflects on his prospects for maintaining a state of grace:

> The snares of the world were its ways of sin. He would fall. He had not yet fallen but he would fall silently, in an instant. Not to fall was too hard, too hard: and he felt the silent lapse of his soul, as it would be at some instant to come, falling, falling but not yet fallen, still unfallen but about to fall. (162)

To interpret the stylistic techniques in these passages as merely extended exercises in rhetoric does not capture the depths of Joyce's insight into the relation between the givenness of experience and the possibilities latent in literary language for expressing various qualities of this giveness. My hypothesis is that we should approach these passages as potential indicators of the extent to which experience can be "mirrored" in language. All three descriptions use repetition, alliteration, assonance, and frequent gerunds and participles. The problem then will be to connect these linguistic devices with the appropriate element or elements within the type of experience described by that language.

Applying the notions of identity and difference to these passages will establish a suitable point of departure. Alliteration and assonance both produce identity of sound within different words. This identity suggests in turn that an element of sameness links the referents of those words, an effect reinforced by the simple repetition of certain words in each description. Gerunds and participles introduce the idea of motion, emphasizing the fact that these experiences as described cannot be mirrored accurately unless their linguistic transcriptions preserve and accentuate the primacy of such motion.

At this point, however, further reflection poses certain problems. Precisely what type of consciousness is described in passage (a)? Is the same type of consciousness described in each of the other two passages? And, similarly, is the motion present in and derivable from the type of consciousness in (a) identical to the motion present in and derivable from the other types of consciousness?

If at the most fundamental metaphysical level the motion of different types of consciousness is the same, then identical stylistic devices can be employed to represent what is, from a metaphysical standpoint, a shared property. But if such motion is not identical, if for example the motion within the consciousness of a nightmarish fantasy differs somehow from the motion within the consciousness of whispered speech, then the extent to which the available language fails to capture this difference is the extent to which such language cannot satisfactorily "mirror" the flow of experience. Can these two types of consciousness be distinguished on the basis of how they are described in the language of *Portrait?* Since the texts cited use virtually identical stylistic devices for both types of consciousness, the relevant distinction seems impossible to establish. And if, in fact, these types of consciousness are distinct in some essential respect, then not only does the structuring of language in *Portrait* fail to distinguish between them, but also it becomes difficult to see how it ever could, given the limits of stylistic innovation in the work as a whole.[3]

There thus remains in *Portrait* a discernible gap between the limits of language and the world beyond language, in particular our consciousness of that world. Unlike *Finnegans Wake,* which expressly indicates that it emerges from a world in which all things are continually in motion, the world of *Portrait* exists according to traditionally fixed boundaries. These boundaries are implicit in the three representative descriptions of consciousness discussed above. And additional evidence of their presence is contained in some of the work's more recognizably metaphysical moments. Consider, for example, space and time. We know of Stephen's awareness of space early in *Portrait* when he turns to the flyleaf of his geography book and reads what has been written there—"himself, his name and where he was"(15).

Stephen Dedalus
Class of Elements
Clongowes Wood College
Sallins
County Kildare
Ireland
Europe
The World
The Universe

The totality of space is evoked in Stephen's consciousness of his whereabouts, but, again unlike the world of the *Wake,* it is a totality differentiated according to classical demarcations.

Language, properly ordered, is fully capable of indicating Stephen's referential connections with all levels of spatial reality. However, language remains subservient to the the objective stability resting in these levels; its semantic limits remain bound to the irreducibly concentric structure of space itself as it appears to an individual existing within that totality.

Given the traditional understanding of space implied in *Portrait,* one might reasonably expect time to be similarly developed. Instead, however, we find time subject to a form of compression which, although not proposed in anything like an objective mode, nonetheless furnishes an intriguing complement to space. When some of Stephen's fellow university students begin to bandy his classical surname about with various Greek case endings, Stephen reacts as follows:

> Their banter was not new to him and now it flattered his mild proud sovereignty. Now, as never before, his strange name seemed to him a prophecy. So timeless seemed the grey warm air, so fluid and impersonal his own mood, that all ages were as one to him. (168)

Stephen's almost mystical union with the fullness of time is accomplished through connotations suggested by his name, as if something about this antique linguistic designator conveyed the power to transcend the limits of the present. However, although the potential unity of "all ages" becomes a palpable reality within the cosmic dimensions of the *Wake,* here in *Portrait* the transcendence of temporal divisions can be little more than the short-lived product of a momentary reverie on a single proper name.

In fact, what is granted to time in the form of a museful possibility is explicitly denied later when Stephen delivers his famous aesthetic theory. One of the necessary conditions of this theory concerns the spatial and temporal considerations which must be met before experience of an aesthetic image becomes possible. Here is the key passage:

> An esthetic image is presented to us either in space or in time. What is audible is presented in time, what is visible is presented in space. But, temporal or spatial, the esthetic image is first luminously apprehended as selfbounded and selfcontained upon the immeasurable background of space or time which is not it. (212)

Before we draw any conclusions from this claim, we should note that Joyce himself may or may not have believed the theory uttered by his spokesman Stephen, and even if he did accept the theory it would still not necessarily follow that all or even some aspects of that theory would have served as part of the implicit metaphysical underpinning of *Portrait* as a whole. For present purposes, however, we should keep in mind the clear distinction between that space or time in which the aesthetic image appears and "the immeasurable background of space or time which is not in it." The assumption is that time must be divisible so that no aesthetic part can exhaust the temporal "background" essential to time's nonaesthetic nature. Thus if the whole of *Portrait* is an "esthetic object," then the principles espoused in *Portrait* itself imply that depthless reaches of time (or space, or both) must exist independently of *Portrait*. As a result, there could be no feasible attempt to incorporate space and time within the language of that aesthetic object, no attempt at a comprehensive self-referential merging of form and content. The vestigial metaphysics in *Portrait* depicts an objective cosmology within which language could never embark on the sort of task demanded of it by the explicit metaphysics of *Finnegans Wake*.

And yet we can conclude by noting several senses in which the language of *Portrait* does possess metaphysical perspectives stretching beyond the limits of the rudimentary metaphysics developed in the work. These again take the form of scattered and apparently unrelated stylistic prefigurements, all occurring toward the conclusion of *Portrait* and hinting even more concretely than preceding sections how language will be developed in Joyce's later work.

Of special prominence is the manipulation of the word "ivy," a process which begins as Stephen's "own consciousness of language was ebbing from his brain and trickling into the very words themselves which set to band and disband themselves in wayward rhythms" (179). "Ivy" thus becomes linked with "ivory," and this conjunction in turn evolves into a meditative medley of synonyms for ivory in other languages. The possibilities of related sound and sense are explored with respect to variations in spelling, all such variations emerging from a single referent and eventually leading back to it through equivalents in different languages. The "wayward rhythms" contained in the initial musings on the word "ivy" are rejected by Stephen as "drivel." Yet these rhythms can be read as structural emblems of what will become an essential process in the linguistic configurations of the *Wake.* The sound of one word generates numerous other words all linked to the first by simple similarity of sound. Such generation is the stimulus for the possibility of intending different and unrelated meanings within one word, and here we find perhaps the tentative genesis of the *Wake* pun.

In addition, the fact that Stephen felt his consciousness "ebbing from his brain and trickling into the very words themselves" attests to the radical centralization of all modes of human awareness within language itself. Language is no longer merely an instrument of consciousness, the latter existing somehow apart from language; rather, the nature of consciousness is now located *within* the peculiar character of words, now understood as employed by consciousness for purposes of defining the very structure of consciousness. Common-sense metaphysics (always of dubious reliability) suggests that consciousness exists prior to language, but the intriguing passage just cited from *Portrait* reverses this relation. And as we know, *Finnegans Wake* will seize this reversal of apparent metaphysical priority and exploit it to the utmost, situating the limits of consciousness by means of the unbounded semantic and referential flow of language.

One of the synonyms Stephen gives for "ivy" is the Latin

ebur, and this supposedly dead language comes to life again a few pages later. The dog Latin interspersed into the conversation between Stephen and Cranly (194–98) illustrates how one "foreign" language can become assimilated into another, assuming of course that it follows the semantic lead of the dominant tongue. The difference between Latin and English remains clearly demarcated at this juncture in *Portrait* (unlike the many linguistic mergers in the *Wake*), but the relevant point is that the inclusion of other languages in the narrative necessarily causes a diversification within the consciousness of both the narrative character and the reader, while at the same time unifying this diversity within the bounds of a single representative of human consciousness. We must know a modicum of Latin in order to comprehend this part of *Portrait,* just as we should know something about many languages in order to have some grasp of the whole of *Finnegans Wake.* In the *Wake,* consciousness will become consciousness of language itself, not, as here in *Portrait,* consciousness of any particular language; nevertheless, *Portrait* in its own muted way points in the direction of this distinctive form of universal awareness.

Finally, the diary form introduced in the last pages of *Portrait* compresses thought and word into an internalized and hence private mode of expression. The consciousness of Stephen Dedalus has been on display throughout the work, but *Portrait* concludes by penetrating the consciousness of its central character at a level where various modes of consciousness are concurrently combined. Once we have reached this level, the difference between what an impersonal external observer relates about a given self and what is hidden within that self begins to blur. The limits of consciousness thus expand through a process of linguistic self-scrutiny, an inverted extension of that very process by which consciousness originally becomes most perspicuously capable of self-expression. As *Portrait* gracefully winds toward its bittersweet and youthfully private conclusion, we are nonetheless en route to the cosmic consciousness of the *Wake.* The various expansions of language —semantic and referential, together with the implicit reduction of different tongues into one—have collectively become part of a process which will reach its fulfillment by engendering a type of consciousness virtually without limits. But the way leading to the realization of this universal consciousness is long and difficult. Linguistic characters of Ulyssean grandeur and proportion are required to continue the exploration of this way.

Ulysses and the Fluidity of Consciousness

A Portrait of the Artist as a Young Man sets in motion the linguistic stream which flows through the currents of consciousness in *Ulysses* and then floods the universe of *Finnegans Wake.* We have just witnessed Stephen Dedalus reflecting on the possibility that language can mirror consciousness. Now if consciousness is defined by some form or forms of motion, then language must somehow incorporate that motion. Let us assume that language mirroring consciousness produces what might be labeled an isomorphism between language and consciousness. Assuming that this isomorphism can at least be approximated if not fully realized, it nonetheless seems clear, as argued in the previous chapter, that *Portrait* falls short of achieving this isomorphism. However, *Portrait* is only an extended moment on the Joycean grand continuum, and much territory remains to be traversed. Therefore the student of Joyce's metaphysics must investigate whether the language of *Ulysses* accomplishes as part of its complex structure the appropriate delineation of motion in consciousness which *Portrait* only hints at and explores only provisionally.

Axiomatic in Joyce criticism is that the eighteen episodes in *Ulysses* exemplify a wide variety of literary styles. Joyce has introduced numerous variations in syntax, word-formation, among other rhetorical devices, presumably to suggest correlations between the texture of the language as read and the experience described as actually experienced. Now the fact that literary styles vary in these structural senses also affects the purely philosophical relations between language and the world, between word as meaningful and word as referential. From the philosophical standpoint, we must then wonder whether the differences between styles lie solely within the domain of language or whether they also point to correlative metaphysical differences in the referential domain of language. For our purposes, the relevant interpretive problem may be posed as follows: can the plurality of styles in *Ulysses* approach what the relative uniformity of style in *Portrait* could not—an isomorphism between language and consciousness?

One might object that raising this question in the context of *Ulysses* lacks suitable critical foundation. Why should a problematic derived from one work be imposed on a completely different work? Why should the tension between the metaphysical demands of *Portrait* and the potential stylistic manifestations of that metaphysics be a factor in interpreting *Ulysses,* especially when we realize that *Ulysses,* unlike both *Portrait* and the *Wake,* seems to avoid explicit discussion of metaphysical issues? But this objection loses its force once one reflects further on the plurality of styles in *Ulysses.* For, evidently, Joyce must achieve something like this isomorphism in order to accomplish at least part of his intention in the work.

We all know that *Ulysses* employs a literary technique referred to as "stream of consciousness," and that it is animated by a variety of stylistic voices. But do the various styles imply that there are different streams of consciousness, or is there just one stream flowing throughout these diversified forms of language? In fact, precisely what does "stream" in the stream of consciousness and how, if at all, is consciousness differentiated by that stream? The diversity of styles in *Ulysses* coupled with the stream of consciousness technique understood as an apparently unitary structure raises questions concerning the nature of consciousness itself—for example, whether or not consciousness can be differentiated into types, and whether language is capable of registering these differentiations. In order to appreciate the scope of *Ulysses'* literary complexity, we are compelled to determine, within feasible limits, how each style relates to the third-person singular narration found in most fiction. By so doing, we will understand more clearly how the variegated language in *Ulysses* evokes a more realistic approximation to the flux of conscious experience.

No grave injustice will be perpetrated against *Ulysses'* literary uniqueness if we consider this complex relation as a circumscribed version of the problem raised by Stephen Dedalus in *Portrait*. Stephen spoke there of the possibility of language mirroring "inner experience." In *Ulysses,* inner experience has become consciousness. And although no character in *Ulysses* wonders about what Stephen had wondered about in *Portrait,* the careful reader must surely continue in this state of wonderment just to be sufficiently knowledgeable about the relation between language and consciousness to understand how the various styles appearing in *Ulysses* fit with one another. Wondering prosaically and philosophically about this relation thus provides the stimulus for this chapter.

Because our inquiry will soon become labyrinthine, we should first establish its most important interpretive and philosophical assumptions. First, we must assume that the literary language of the stream of consciousness can reveal at least part of the nature of consciousness; second, we must also assume that this language will elucidate the structure of consciousness at a level transcending the particular consciousness belonging to this or that individual. In short, at least part of what we read about Bloom and Molly must be characteristic of Everyman—if not, then there are no grounds for claiming that whatever linguistically represents their stream of consciousness can be construed as indicative of the nature of consciousness in a broader sense.

These assumptions concern the relation between consciousness and literary language purporting to disclose the nature of consciousness. However, additional assumptions come into play for that particular form of literary language peculiar to *Ulysses*. For example, we shall assume that a difference in style implies, or at least suggests, some kind of difference in type of consciousness. This assumption is especially crucial, since it presupposes that consciousness can be distinguished into types which can somehow be represented through variations in language. We should bear in mind that there may be no such thing as a "pure" type of consciousness existing in a state unmixed with some other type or types. Also, some types of consciousness (or some aspects of all types of consciousness) may resist literary representation. Experience of these types may remain ineffable, yet not for that reason be any less real, to the individual who experiences them. Finally, even if we can isolate various types of consciousness, the relation between any given stream of consciousness and its literary representations may be only accidental. In other words, it may be that the same aspect of consciousness can be evoked in different ways by different stylistic devices. This possibility would not detract from the achievement of *Ulysses,* if achievement it turns out to be; rather, it merely attests to the fact that *Ulysses* has not spoken the last word in revealing the convoluted structure of consciousness through literary representation.

The sheer multiplicity of styles in *Ulysses* presents additional problems for organizing a critical inquiry of this sort. One might take an inordinate number of approaches to situating this rich work along the same continuum with the *Wake*. Thus we can only mention here certain intriguing anticipations of techniques employed in the *Wake*. For example, observe the introduction of language with a predominantly visual function during the Aeolus episode, as when the headline "K.M.R.I.A." prefaces Myles Crawford's loud cry, "He can kiss my royal Irish arse" (147.10). The reader is intended to see the initials of this Celtic crudity in newspaper print concurrently with the full expression of that crudity, just as in the *Wake* we will see the letter E gyrating with its own special spatial sense. Yet another anticipation of the language of the *Wake* is found in a locution such as "*Entweder* transsubstantiality *oder* consubstantiality but in no case subsubstantiality" (391.40–41), which incorporates a foreign language and playful alteration of Latinate prefixes for purposes of irony. Both techniques, when expanded and refined, become vital to the *Wake.* Finally, consider Bloom's question, "What anagrams had he made on his name in youth?" He answers himself:

> Leopold Bloom
> Ellpodbomool
> Molldopeloob.
> Bollopedoom
> Old Ollebo, M.P. (678.12–17)

These rearrangements of the letters in a proper name have been executed not merely for the sake of their euphonious juxtaposition, but also to generate humorous linguistic perspectives on the individual Bloom through alteration of what linguistically represents his identity, his name. It is not difficult to see how the same principle could be imaginatively broadened and applied not just to proper names, but to any word capable of being semantically and referentially expanded by such ingenuity.

These and other stylistic devices foreshadowing techniques employed in the *Wake* could be given additional scrutiny from a literary-philosophical perspective. However, the particular angle of interpretation I have selected for consideration in this chapter—the potential isomorphism between language and consciousness—is more than sufficiently complex. And even this interpretation must be limited in view of the number of approaches yet possible.[1] For example, we have noted that the linguistic terrain of *Ulysses* as a whole is characterized by numerous styles. Now if some of these styles are stream of consciousness, then we might inventory them to determine whether they share one or several properties. We could compare these properties with the relevant features of *Portrait* and *Finnegans Wake* to locate the structural similarities and differences among the three works. However, although such a procedure has the obvious merit of comprehensiveness, it would soon become apparent that examining the content of all possible stream of consciousness styles would make it difficult to determine the relevant properties common to *Ulysses*. As we shall see, Joyce's literary development of consciousness is extremely subtle and intricate, so that the ideal of universal treatment must be sacrificed for a more manageable goal.

And such a goal is not without merit, both literary and philosophical. I have chosen to construe *Ulysses* as implicitly posing a series of fundamental questions concerning the relation between language and human consciousness, ultimately between language and being, insofar as consciousness exemplifies one part of being. From the standpoint of metaphysics, we shall concentrate on the problem of the primacy of flux, in particular by trying to identify different types of consciousness as they become present within linguistic transcriptions.[2] This line of interpretation will, to some degree, cut across what has become the typical classification of *Ulysses* into episodes, rhetorical methods, etc., as outlined in, say, Gilbert's well-known study.[3] But the distinctive philosophical demands of the projected inquiry should compensate for any critical disorientation which might result for the student of Joyce, since it will become evident that *Ulysses* is a literary work well worth careful philosophical scrutiny. In fact, if we assume that the fabric of human consciousness is intrinsically complex, then it may well be that *Ulysses* explores this aspect of reality more profoundly than does the *Wake*'s treatment of the intricate metaphysics of perpetual flux.

As examples of Joyce's style in *Ulysses*, I will cite four excerpts from the novel, then paraphrase and comment on the scope and types of consciousness treated in each one. Once we examine these excerpts in close conjunction with one another, their diversity should impress on us even more forcefully the need to scrutinize the "stream of consciousness" method to discern, for example, identity and difference within the boundaries of the possible isomorphism between language and consciousness.

(1) Bloom concludes his trip to Dublin's public baths:

> There's Hornblower standing at the porter's lodge. Keep him on hands: might take a turn in there on the nod. How do you do, Mr Hornblower? How do you do, sir?
>
> Heavenly weather really. If life was always like that. Cricket weather. Sit around under sunshades. Over after over. Out. They can't play it here. Duck for six wickets. Still Captain Buller broke a window in the Kildare street club with a slog to square leg. Donnybrook fair more in their line. And the skulls we were acracking when M'Carthy took the floor. Heatwave. Won't last. Always passing, the stream of life, which in the stream of life we trace is dearer than them all.
>
> Enjoy a bath now: clean trough of water, cool enamel, the gentle tepid stream. This is my body. (86.23–35)

Bloom sees Hornblower, but present visual perception quickly veers into an imaginative state of affairs taking place in a possible future. Then perception changes from vision alone to vision and touch. This complex form of perception fades into general musings about life, but rapidly returns to the concrete particularity of cricket, with thoughts ranging from ruminations about the game in general to the memory of a particular event in the local history of the game. A musical evocation captures some of the rhythm of the game and continues the associations of the past with the present, this time between aural memory of a popular tune and present reflection on an imaginary cricket match. The tactile perception of heat takes over, but is soon replaced by a weather forecast, again mixing present perception with a form of nonperceptual cognition about the future. Tactility then becomes imaginative, connecting the transience of felt experience to the transience of all experience. The liquid element in the image expressing transience carries Bloom's consciousness from the vicinity of the porter's lodge to the public baths, where the image becomes a tactile representation of Bloom in contact with water and enamel. His final thoughts join the physical referent of these experiences, his body, to another body, this one belonging to Christ, an exemplar of dying to the flesh altogether.

There are several distinct types of consciousness introduced in this passage—sense perception (visual, aural, tactile), memory, and imagination. Yet it is possible to question whether Bloom's consciousness "streams" at all, at least at this point. Both the style of the language and the content of each linguistic unit are discontinuous, marked by sudden pauses and equally sudden shifts in intention. It is, in fact, virtually impossible to tell that consciousness is differentiated into types unless we attend to what the language says—the periodic style alone does not indicate this. We also must note that the continuity of consciousness is controlled just as much by Bloom's imagination and memory as by what he sees in the space-time of living perception. Given the scope of Bloom's awareness, we can readily determine the reasons for the transitions between any two stages of consciousness. However, Bloom's consciousness at this point seems to be in a state of random flux in the sense that what appears linguistically within his conscious attention merely incorporates whatever has made the most palpable impression on him. The desultory, continually shifting language reflects this state.

(2) Shortly thereafter, many thoughts pass through Bloom's mind as the body of his friend Patrick Dignam is about to be lowered into the ground:

> Shades of night hovering here with all the dead stretched about. The shadows of the tombs when churchyards yawn and Daniel O'Connell must be a descendant I suppose who is this used to say he was queer breedy man great catholic all the same like a big giant in the dark. Will o' the wisp. Gas of graves. Want to keep her mind off it to conceive at all. Woman especially are so touchy.
> (108.3–9)

The passage begins on a very literary note; Bloom's somewhat lyrical observation could be an impersonal narrative account of what one might experience in a cemetery at night.

However, the next sentence is intricately suggestive of consciousness at its most streaming. Bloom sees the shadows of the tombs and is instantly reminded of a salient image from *Hamlet,* his consciousness quickly moving from raw perception to involuted memory and imagination. But then he notices the tomb of a specific individual, apparently related to someone whom Bloom and the funeral entourage had just been discussing, and he conjectures on the possible blood relation between the two. Such speculation fades away as he sees something else, probably another tomb, one bearing the bones of an unknown deceased. But the known takes precedence over the unknown, and Bloom returns to report what had been voiced concerning the living relation of the deceased. Visual perception then becomes imaginative again in separate (and alliterative) evocations of a shadowy graveyard viewed at night. The sight of dead men flashes to the memory of living women, in particular their natural capacity for conceiving new life and, according to Bloom's ruminations, their equally natural reaction to the process in general. Once more, the present purely visual field has faded before associations held in Bloom's memory and evaluative judgments based on these memories.

The lengthy sentence in the center of this passage is doubtless its most arresting feature. What does this sentence, lacking internal punctuation, imply about consciousness? And does the fact that it is both preceded and followed by periodic reflections, styled as in passage (1), say something essential about consciousness? If we assume that the primary avenue of consciousness represented in passages (1) and (2) is perceptual, then it would seem to follow that perception is fragmented in (1) but fluid in (2) either because the objects Bloom sees differ from one another or because some aspect in Bloom's perceptual consciousness generates fluidity in the one case but fragmentation in the other. Can these possibilities be narrowed and analyzed more precisely? Let us consider another passage.

(3) Bloom has just slipped into a "half-dream" after his vicarious erotic interlude while in the presence of the lame Gerty Caffrey:

> O sweety all your little girlwhite up I saw dirty bracegirdle made me do love sticky we two naughty Grace darling she him half past the bed met him pike hoses frillies for Raoul to perfume your wife black hair heave under embon *señorita* young eyes Mulvey plump years dreams return tail end Agendath swoony lovey showed me her next year in drawers return next in her next her next. (382.13–19)

Bloom's half dream begins with his visualizing a portion of Gerty's clothing, then shifts quickly to a description in appropriately pubescent language depicting the effect this sight had on him. The identity of Bloom's unknowing female partner flits rapidly from Gerty to Grace darling (a lighthouse keeper's valorous daughter) to Molly and her attempt to pronounce Greek. Several excerpts from the book Bloom had purchased for his wandering wife surround an explicit mention of Molly and one of her most striking physical features, her hair. Thus, the memory of the recent past has slid into a more distant past, and Bloom's consciousness becomes gradually more compressed and repetitive. Gerty and Molly then mingle with a single Hebrew word and a phrase found in a prayer from the Passover Service. Could it be that Bloom's Semitic conscience is making its presence felt?

Here we find jumbled phrases and single words, the result mixing past and present, memory and imagination, sight and touch. It is selective, discrete, and fragmentary. Notice that from a purely stylistic standpoint, passages (2) and (3) are identical in lacking punctuation. Is it possible that the intensity of a recent orgasm as dreamt is stylistically indistinguishable from the continuity of perceiving a tombstone? Surely such diverse forms of consciousness will differ in some respects. In order to draw the appropriate distinctions from these texts, we must compare the stream of passage (2) with that of (3). Observe that the transitions in (2) are more controlled than those in (3), and that there are discernibly different tempi in the two passages, with (3) much more *accelerando* than (2). Might we then infer that dream consciousness is intrinsically more unstable than perceptual consciousness? But if so, then can the discontinuity within the process of dreaming be established linguistically so that it can be clearly distinguished from the discontinuity of visual perception? These and other related questions will become even more pressing after we consider the final passage.

(4) This excerpt is drawn from Molly's monologue, the remarkable coda to *Ulysses:*

> Yes because he never did a thing like that before as ask to get his breakfast in bed with a couple of eggs since the *City Arms* Hotel when he used to be pretending to be laid up with a sick voice doing his highness to make himself interesting to that old faggot Mrs Riordan that he thought he had a great leg of and she never left us a farthing all for masses for herself and her soul greatest miser ever was . . . there was no love lost between us thats 1 consolation I wonder what kind is that book he brought me Sweets of Sin by a gentleman of fashion some other Mr de Kock I suppose the people gave him that nickname going about with his tube from one woman to another I couldnt even change my new white shoes all ruined with the saltwater and the hat I had with that feather all blowy and tossed on me how annoying and provoking because the smell of the sea excited me of course the sardines and the bream in Catalan bay round the back of the rock they were fine all silver in the fishermens baskets old Luigi near a hundred they said came from Genoa and the tall old chap with the earrings I dont like a man you have to climb up to go get at . . . and how he kissed me under the Moorish wall and I thought well as well him as another and then I asked him with my eyes to ask again yes and then he asked me would I yes to say yes my mountain flower and first I put my arms around him yes and drew him down to me so he could feel my breasts all perfume yes and his heart was going like mad and yes I said yes I will Yes. (738.1–7, 765.9–21, 783.8–14)

Molly opens her disquisition by affirming something, "Yes," although precisely what she says "yes" to is not immediately evident (perhaps the concluding lines contain a clue). She first registers her discontent with the now adjacent and supine Bloom by recalling a past incident when Bloom had acted in a way offensive to Molly's womanly sensibilities. Her negativity then spreads from Bloom to the erstwhile target of Bloom's affection, Mrs. Riordan, who died without leaving the Blooms a farthing. Molly's present consciousness is filled with memories split into recent and more remote past. Later, Molly concludes another remembered episode by declaiming forthrightly, if somewhat tritely, her relations to Bloom at that time, punctuating this portion of her thoughts by substituting the arabic number 1 for the word "one" (a device occurring frequently in the monologue), as if her consolations had been conceived on the model of an arithmetical exercise. She links memories of her general relations to Bloom to the book Bloom had just brought her, slipping quickly from memory into an imaginative explanation for the author's less than subtle name. Imagination is again replaced by memory as the connotative force of that name returns Molly to her own carnality. But she is not entirely narcissistic; her memory of new white shoes and hat slides into places and people she had seen when she wore them. Here too, however, an apparently neutral memory climaxes in a statement of preference in matters sexual, presumably an attitude based on past experience and extending through the present and into the future. The finale is an intimate memory of Molly's sexual initiation, with her fluid and frequent "Yes" expressing approval, and doubtless something more, of what had happened then, thus combining in circular fashion the first word of her monologue with the last as if the whole event were a kind of world unto itself.

Molly's disquisition is a unity to the same degree that any self-contained flux is a unity, but it becomes differentiable as soon as one recognizes that sometimes the flux is moved by imagination, sometimes by memory. (This claim and all subsequent discussion concerns only the excerpts cited, not the entire monologue.) But even within the bounds of introspection, should the flow of memory be rendered stylistically in a manner identical to the flow of imagination? Surely not, for it would then become virtually impossible to distinguish the two types of consciousness as they appear in language.

This problem becomes more prominent, and correlatively more decisive metaphysically, if Molly's introspection branches out into additional regions of human consciousness. On the assumption that the style of Molly's discourse is uniformly structured, then the more different types of consciousness present to that discourse, the more difficult it will be to preserve these differences within the undifferentiated flux of a common linguistic form. Furthermore, the same problem arises if the interplay of memory and imagination here in passage (4) is compared with the transcription of the consciousness of perception found in (2). We have thus three qualitatively distinct types of consciousness, and it would seem that an isomorphic representation in language would guarantee that these differences be discernibly preserved. But both passages (2) and (4), whether viewed stylistically or semantically, seem to flow within the same forms of linguistic motion. We may provisionally conclude that for all its manifest complexity and diversity, the style of *Ulysses* seems destined to fall short of the goal hypothesized in *Portrait*—the potential mirroring of consciousness in language.

Discussion

As I have noted, my interpretive approach to *Ulysses* has been suggested by a possibility abstracted from *Portrait*. We have been examining the language of *Ulysses* to determine the sense in which an isomorphism, an identity of sorts, has been realized between language and human consciousness. However, while its stylistic variety takes considerable strides toward reaching this identity, *Ulysses* nonetheless still falls short, although it is difficult to say precisely why. Even if an ingenious use of language can approximate an isomorphism with the particular "feel" of consciousness as actually experienced, the metaphysical fact remains that language about a given type of consciousness must remain distinct from consciousness itself. Seeing a tombstone and describing the visual perception of a tombstone are not the same. Therefore, any approximate realization of this isomorphism must indicate how language and consciousness differ, while at the same time it conveys the requisite sense in which they are the same. The metaphysical phase of our study of the treatment of consciousness in *Ulysses* will thus not be complete until we seek to determine the limits of what might be referred to as the expressibility of language, how close language can come to imitating the distinctive textures of consciousness. Thus in addition to interpretation, we must attempt to discern the conditions to be met before an author can approximate the isomorphism in question.

How do the streams of stylized language in *Ulysses* evoke the streaming of consciousness itself? We must remember that stream of consciousness in *Ulysses* includes several different phases in the actual process of consciousness streaming. By isolating the properties pertaining to consciousness and their primary features, we should be able to recognize more clearly what language must do in order to approach a degree of parity with the living presence of consciousness. From the four passages in *Ulysses* examined above, we may derive the following primary properties:

(a) Consciousness always intends some kind of object, whether that object be perceptibly observable in space and time or imperceptibly present within the internal domains of imagining, remembering, dreaming, etc. Thus Bloom sees a porter, remembers a sport, wishes for a pleasanter lot in life, dreams about nubile females, feels warm water on his body. And Molly's consciousness intends an enormous variety of objects in this technical sense of the term, even though in her reverie she perceives none of them as such. Occasionally the precise nature of the object of consciousness may be difficult to specify—some of the referents in the rapid perception described in passage (2) illustrate this feature. But it is undeniable that referents exist, even if their identity may never be known outside the particular locus of consciousness in which they appear.

(b) Thus if consciousness streams, it does so in the process of apprehending some object (both terms understood in a very wide sense). This stream will necessarily include some aspect of all those objects which participate in its intrinsic flux-like character.

(c) Furthermore, the stream of consciousness can be distinguished into different types. Bloom perceiving a young female differs from Bloom fantasizing about her, and both types of consciousness differ from Bloom in a dreaming reverie mixing fact and fancy concerning the same intentional object.

(d) However, saying that consciousness always intends an object and is deployed into types is not saying enough. Note, for example, that a given type of consciousness exhibits a stable pattern between individual consciousness and the object of that consciousness. This pattern is essential to preserve the character of a particular type of consciousness as being of one type and not of some other type. Thus Bloom's floating memory of his onanistic union with Gerty may be fleeting, but while it lasts it is this type of consciousness, that is, memory, and no other. There is nonetheless an element of process *within* each type of consciousness, and thus it makes sense to assert that consciousness always streams even when it has been categorized in a certain manner.

(e) All such types of consciousness have only limited duration. These periods vary from the brevity of Bloom's daydreaming to the marathon length of Molly's introspective odyssey.

(f) Although each type of consciousness streams, it would be premature to assume that each type streams in the same way as any other type. All rivers run, but not all at the same rate, and the tempo of language in the passages cited above attests to this difference. The process of Bloom perceiving an object and remembering the same object will differ, even though the individual consciousness and the object of that consciousness are identical in both cases.

(g) Consciousness seems to be intrinsically unstable in that any one of its types eventually gives way to another. Furthermore, this discontinuity is random—from a given direction or locus, consciousness can veer and shift into any one of many other types without any rational link or transition.

(h) Thus consciousness streams in another sense. For there is fluctuation not only *within* one type of consciousness but also *between* different types of consciousness, as between Bloom musing and Bloom perceiving. Therefore, a consciousness streams when intending a given object within one type of consciousness and when shifting between (and among) different types of consciousness and concomitant variations in intentional objects.

The above outline, which I will use as my working definition of "stream of consciousness," is not intended to represent *all* the complexities of the stream of consciousness technique as found in *Ulysses*. It is sufficient to have demonstrated that the stream is multiple, that it meanders as it flows, and that it is complex. Once granting this complexity, we are justified in questioning whether language is capable of depicting the elements of flux within any one type of consciousness, capturing the shift between different types of consciousness, or illustrating the difference between the flux of one type of consciousness and that of another. Literary style must accomplish these various representations in order that the isomorphism between language and consciousness can be approximated, if not fully realized. Of course, the fact that one can derive these properties from the language of *Ulysses* does not necessarily imply that language is capable of such representation. The structures of consciousness thus referred to may be presented so that the meanings and referents of words will not provide the qualitative diversity essential for the proposed isomorphism. And, in fact, there are good reasons to believe that this isomorphism has not been achieved. These reasons, as interesting as they are intricate, become fundamental not only to understanding the function of the stream of consciousness in *Ulysses* but also, as we shall see, to connecting this important aspect of *Ulysses* with the world of *Finnegans Wake*.

Once we have examined the four passages cited above in somewhat greater critical detail, the purely theoretical relation between consciousness and its objects will assume greater literary and philosophical importance. The following commentaries provide a conceptual measure for gauging the degree to which the isomorphism between language and consciousness has been achieved. These commentaries constitute a set of variations illustrating the crucial emergence of identity and difference within the metaphysical structure of the isomorphism.

Passage (1), Bloom reflecting on a cricket match in progress and feeling his bath water, blends imagination and tactile perception with several fragmented visual inferences based on these various cues. Now the periodic punctuation in this passage does not, by itself, provide a clue for distinguishing stylistically among what may be assumed as three types of consciousness—touch, vision, and imagination. Nor is there any apparent source of distinction in the way language itself has evoked these types. Thus essentially the same linguistic style has been employed for evident shifts among different types of consciousness. How then can there be an identity between just one form of language and such uniquely different types of consciousness? It seems clear that the requisite isomorphic differences cannot be preserved.

Passage (2), Bloom in the cemetery, also originates with perception, although here vision seems to dominate to the exclusion of the other senses. And as in passage (1), Bloom's perception mingles with his imagination. But the transition in passage (2) from perception to imagination is marked by a lack of punctuation while the same transition in passage (1) includes punctuation. What in the nature of the shift between these different types of consciousness justifies this stylistic difference? Is Bloom's perception of a porter qualitatively different from his perception of a tombstone? The two different stream of consciousness styles suggest that they are different, but how can we be certain? For if the two perceptual events do in fact flow from the same type of consciousness, then these stylistic differences will surely distort somewhat the unity of that form of streaming consciousness.

Passage (3), Bloom reliving a moment of fluid ecstasy, resembles the second sentence of (2) in that both lack punctuation. And yet the types of consciousness manifested by these passages are clearly different. The most obvious stylistic variant derives from the relative speed at which different entities referentially appear and disappear. The rate of change is much slower in (2) than it is in (3). But does the tempo of these passages offer sufficient ground for distinguishing a type of fluid visual perception from a state of half-dreaming? Or does the difference depend on the degree of randomness exemplified by the transitions marking the changes from one referent to another? Again, it is difficult to answer these questions just from the content of the passages.

Passage (4), from Molly's soliloquy, is characterized by an absence of punctuation, as is part of (2) and all of (3). This characteristic is a ready stylistic device for evoking flux, but here too the problem remains of locating some means for distinguishing among different types of flowing consciousness. If, for the sake of simplicity, Molly's state of consciousness is designated as a self-conscious mixture of memory and imagination, then we may well wonder what distinguishes the flux of this conjunctive type of introspective activity from a counterpart episode such as the rendition of Bloom's reflections in (2). But the most difficult problem is to divide the rampaging flux of Molly's own discourse into distinguishable types of consciousness. For within this discourse there are various types of consciousness, a variety only hinted at in the stylistic development quoted in passage (4). Molly remembers, resents, wishes, evaluates, etc. But how can the mere lack of punctuation, or even divergences in the amount of language she devotes to her various referential interests, capture the essential differences between and among these types of consciousness?

This problem, arising from reflection on the structure of Molly's monologue, is compounded when we juxtapose the seeming boundlessness of the consciousness surveyed there with, for example, the characterizations of consciousness in passages (2) and (3). On the basis of variations in language alone, it is difficult to distinguish between Bloom's visual consciousness in

(2) and Molly's primarily nonvisual consciousness in (4), or between Bloom's half-dream reverie in (3) and, again, Molly's wide-awake ruminations. The referents of Molly's thoughts do not shift as jerkily as Bloom's, thus indicating that the waking Molly exerts more control over the succession of her thoughts than the dozing Bloom, and we could perhaps use this control as a necessary condition for distinguishing half-dream consciousness from introspective waking consciousness. But this characteristic is hardly sufficient, since rational waking introspection can change its objects of attention at great speed, if such is its purpose, and half-dreaming consciousness occasionally lingers over one or several intended objects.

These problems imply that the isomorphism between language and consciousness has been approached but not realized in *Ulysses*. This conclusion may be restated in appropriate metaphysical terminology—the stream of consciousness narrative method is so complex that the differentiation provided by *Ulysses'* multiform styles remains inadequate for generating the desired identity. But can we explain why the convoluted language of *Ulysses* has missed the relevant metaphysical mark?

In general, a linguistic unit can be seen to evoke a given type of consciousness in flux if it is possible to coordinate elements of language with elements of the type of consciousness to be evoked. Furthermore, we have seen that each type of consciousness may be divided into two poles—the flow of consciousness itself and the object of consciousness intended by that flux. Now it is true that Joyce has taken a stand of sorts on one of these poles, the flux-character of consciousness. But this fact alone, viewed metaphysically, is not sufficient to determine whether a given instance of language can properly mirror this aspect of consciousness. For example, we do not yet know whether the flux of consciousness is orderly, disorderly, or sometimes either one. Is the flux constituted so that we can somehow determine its function within different types of consciousness? Do different types of consciousness actualize different types of flux? We find no answers to such questions in *Ulysses*. Yet we must answer them if we are to discover when and how language should stipulate or evoke ordered flux, disordered flux, or other modes of consciousness.

In addition to the flow of consciousness is the intended object of consciousness. Now it seems reasonable that if consciousness always intends an object, then all objects of consciousness will be continually changing insofar as they are objects *of consciousness,* or insofar as they become an integral part of the very process of streaming consciousness. Presumably it also follows that the linguistic transcription of consciousness in flux would depict the object of consciousness as somehow part of that flux. At this point, however, we must recall that the metaphysical status of *all* objects of consciousness in the world of *Ulysses* has been left in silence and thus is indeterminate. We know that consciousness must stream forth, but we know nothing about the metaphysical character of all possible objects of consciousness.

It would, of course, be premature to infer that all objects of consciousness must themselves be in perpetual flux simply because they can participate in the processes of consciousness. For objects of consciousness may be themselves impervious to this stream, or at least left essentially unaffected by it. Thus a tombstone as object of perception fluctuates in the sense that its shape is presented perspectivally to a moving observer, but the tombstone itself can hardly be said to be in flux for this reason. The point is that the metaphysical status of a potential object of consciousness must be investigated and described precisely as an object of consciousness to determine the extent to which it is affected by being a party to the perceptual process. And *Ulysses* leaves us without guidance on this pivotal matter.

The more regions of reality that become present as objects of consciousness, the more this multiplicity affects how consciousness and its objects form a unified whole—a stream of consciousness. And if, as a theoretical possibility, human consciousness can become aware of totality, then there is all the more reason to acknowledge the fact that the unspecified structure of the objects intended by consciousness does not allow us to decide whether or not the linguistic representation of the stream of consciousness has captured the qualitative texture of a given type of consciousness in conjunction with its intended object. It seems that all versions of stream of consciousness language in *Ulysses* take their stylistic cue from what might be termed the subjective pole of the consciousness/object relation, thus virtually ignoring any possible sense in which the object of consciousness could affect the metaphysical character of this relation. As a result, the potential isomorphism between language and consciousness suffers from the fact that an integral aspect of streaming consciousness—the metaphysical nature of its objects—has gone without attention.

If the structures of both poles of streaming consciousness are either unanalyzed or left without sufficient specification, then the sense in which a given linguistic unit represents a given type of consciousness depends solely on our intuitive feel that one sort of language elicits that type of consciousness more finely than another sort of language. For instance, an exercise in self-scrutiny during a leisurely stroll may verify that our consciousness attends to various objects for various lengths of time, never dwelling for long on any one, never probing beyond immediate impressions of what has been perceived. A linguistic representation of this type of consciousness, such as in passage (2), coordinates well with this description. But surely the persuasiveness of this representation ultimately depends not on what "feels" correct, but on a detailed reflective analysis of the relevant state, in particular the general properties predicated of that state. In this and all other stream of consciousness passages in *Ulysses*, however, there are no explicitly designated structures of reality which exist apart from language and against which a purely stylistic configuration can be compared for purposes of establishing and measuring a potential isomorphism. The accuracy with which each stylistic description mirrors a type of consciousness thus rests, perhaps precariously, on a correspondence between a "feel" for complex literary language and some intuitive sense that this feeling accurately and comprehensively evokes the type of consciousness intended by the language under examination.

It may be useful at this point to situate the above discussion in light of the Joycean continuum as a whole. The key notion of a possibly illuminating isomorphism between language and consciousness was derived from an important passage in *Portrait.* The application of that notion to *Ulysses* established an interpretive ground on which it was possible to recognize and explore crucial metaphysical considerations with respect to the relation between language and consciousness, in particular the correlation between a certain mode of streaming literary language and the essential character of streaming consciousness as such. The analysis of this common ground will eventually point the way toward realizing how the designated connections between *Portrait* and *Ulysses* lead to an appropriately philosophical and literary appreciation of *Finnegans Wake.* As a prelude to that transition, however, we can assert some tentative conclusions concerning the import of this line of thought on the complex structure of *Ulysses* as a distinct moment on the Joycean continuum.

Our brief venture into the metaphysics of consciousness has revealed that even the variegated language of *Ulysses* falls short of approximating the apparent structure of consciousness as flux. To regard this judgment as of more philosophical than literary interest is premature, and overlooks the possibility that what we may assume to be the purely literary dimension of the stream of consciousness technique in *Ulysses* cannot be accurately surveyed without investigating the metaphysical character of the referents of this language. This essential connection between implicit metaphysics and the ultimate significance of literary style should become even more palpable once we reflect further on an intriguing, perhaps even paradoxical, characteristic of the stylistic structure of *Ulysses* as a whole.

Assume for the sake of argument that Joyce's insights into the relation between language and consciousness have established the isomorphism in question. Thus each of the various stylistic treatments of the stream of consciousness can be seen to reproduce the exact feel of consciousness as actually experienced. But *Ulysses* is not written entirely in stream of consciousness style. The very first episode, for example, is written in standard third-person narrative prose. What are the implicit metaphysical properties of the consciousness animating the concealed personality underlying this classic narrative schematic? The nameless narrator of this and other episodes in the work is impersonal, of fixed character, with unflinchingly stable attitudes—a pure observer of events completely external to the concerns of his (her?) consciousness. Presumably the entire world grounding the narrator's perspective on all the events so described is similarly fixed. Thus the most prosaic of the styles in *Ulysses* would be based on a metaphysical stance which, insofar as it rests on stability, is set apart from the metaphysics of the stream of consciousness as found in those characters through whom this aspect of reality is revealed.

Upon reflection, the literary import of the metaphysical ground for third-person narration becomes evident: it is precisely the stability of this narrative style which establishes distance between the relatively fixed metaphysics surrounding the nameless narrator and the perpetual flux of consciousness. We perhaps too readily overlook the fact that *Ulysses* does not confront its reader with *continual* stream of consciousness technique, and the other styles used represent a locus of fixed—if unspecified—referents from which we may secure our bearings once consciousness begins to stream forth. We note then that the literary totality of *Ulysses* displays extended periods of fixity entirely absent from that world referentially defined by the metaphysics of *Finnegans Wake*. This suggestive comparison can be developed both for the relation between *Ulysses* and *Finnegans Wake* and, our present concern, for comprehending *Ulysses* as a complex whole.

We are now in a position to appreciate how the quality of motion in the stream of consciousness narrative technique, as used in *Ulysses*, in conjunction with the static character grounding the impersonal narrator, forces an intriguing metaphysical problem with significant critical and literary repercussions. The problem may be phrased as follows: if consciousness is always in a state of flux and if the narration of observed events is one kind of conscious act, then such narration should exhibit the flux essential to all types of consciousness. However, in direct contrast to the inherent fluidity of the stream of consciousness, the fixed character of the third-person narrator introduces an apparently irreducible stability into the metaphysics of consciousness, implicitly but also undeniably. As a result, *Ulysses* contains mixed modes of consciousness, one essentially in motion when represented within the stream of consciousness styles, and one essentially at rest when it forms the stark background for the impersonal narration of external events—yet how is such a heterodox mixture possible if consciousness itself displays metaphysical unity? Consciousness can come to rest only when its necessary flow has been halted by an apparently arbitrary selection of attitudinal perspectives which then assume equal status with the totality of consciousness. One might legitimately contend that the implicit metaphysics of the third-person narrative style depends on a truncated distortion of the full complexity of consciousness as it has been revealed in the appropriate stream of consciousness episodes.

Once the styles in *Ulysses* begin to oscillate between standard prose narrative and stream of consciousness narrative, an unavoidable metaphysical tension emerges between a world essentially defined by motion and an overlapping world characterized in part by rest. However, one might still object that this tension, however real, remains strictly philosophical in character. After all, there is hardly an equivalent tension in the overall literary structure of the work. Are there any literary reasons for criticizing the structure of *Ulysses* simply because of the variation between ordinary prose style and stream of consciousness techniques? Surely, one might continue, this difference is purely literary, independent of such metaphysical tangles.

But the situation is more complex. The stream of consciousness style and the standard style of prose narration, while differing widely as vehicles of literary meaning, must nonetheless preserve some measure of semantic identity insofar as both refer to the same range of entities. To grasp the rich complexity of the stream of consciousness technique, we have had to analyze its constituent parts, especially the intricate relation between the meaning of stream of consciousness language and the objects it refers to and which stimulated it. This inquiry has explained how this type of language and this form of consciousness are correlated, both semantically and referentially. But surely we could approach the language of "traditional" prose style in the same way, since it is no less permeated with implicit metaphysics than stream of consciousness style. Thus if determining the literary structure of stream of consciousness styles presupposes an excursus into the metaphysics of consciousness, and particularly into the relation between language and the structure of that metaphysics, then perhaps we should also investigate the literary structure of traditional prose style.

Of course, the literary tension emerging from the presence of widely contrasting narrative styles within the same work is perhaps not as pressing for resolution as is its metaphysical counterpart. For the metaphysician, a description of reality based on principles of continual flux cannot coexist with another description of reality based on principles of stability; however, for the literary critic, diversity of style merely reflects varied viewpoints, particularly in the work of a master craftsman. If our lack of inquiry into the relation between all the various styles of traditional literary language and human consciousness can be overlooked, then we will continue interpreting the products of such literary representation without concerning ourselves with the apparently more abstract factors through which these styles have become traditional. But if the metaphysical tension is real and must be resolved, can its literary counterpart be ignored? Can a critic be sufficiently knowledgeable to evaluate the structure of stream of consciousness technique without knowing at least something of the metaphysics underlying the structure of traditional literary language?

Consider this hypothetical possibility as a locus for reflection relevant both to an understanding of *Ulysses* and for establishing a return to *Finnegans Wake*. From the standpoint of metaphysics, the problematic tension just outlined would have been at least confronted if, at some point in the narrative, *Ulysses* had taken a stand on the defining characteristics of whatever mode of reality underlies both consciousness and the intentional objects of consciousness. Of course, the mere appearance of this metaphysical dimension somewhere within the work should not, by its mere presence, have answered all the relevant questions concerning the relation between language and consciousness, but it would have situated the treatment of consciousness and its objects on an appropriately comprehensive metaphysical plane.

Now in this regard, it is vital to note that *Finnegans Wake* does take such a stand on precisely this level of abstraction, a forthright stand frequently voiced. Part I of this study has shown that the *Wake* is based, in part, on a vividly descriptive metaphysical substructure. This abstract configuration conveys the senses in which flux permeates all reality—mental, physical, historical, logical. By comparison, flux in *Ulysses* is restricted to that portion of the narrative which attempts to evoke the living reality of consciousness. Furthermore, this attempt receives no visible metaphysical support in the text of the work, whether within the flow of consciousness or outside it. The responsibility is left to the reader to determine the sense in which the language of the narrative has taken this particular turn. On the other hand, the flux of consciousness as it streams forth in *Finnegans Wake* has been extended to encompass all reality, an extension warranted by the explicit metaphysical doctrine interspersed throughout the work. We have been at pains to emphasize that the reader who misses this philosophical underpinning and its effect on the language of the *Wake* has overlooked a substantial factor in the cosmology of *Finnegans Wake*.

This comparison of the status and scope of flux in *Ulysses* and the *Wake* may epitomize our brief excursus into the two major prose works preceding *Finnegans Wake*. Part II of this study has been intended both as a natural outgrowth of the kind of inquiry pursued in part I and as a metaphysical prerequisite for the type of analysis to be attempted in part III. For it will be the major burden of the last part to demonstrate that the problems raised here concerning the explicit and implicit metaphysical components of *Portrait* and *Ulysses* can, if properly extended and modified, serve as a critical framework for assessing the complex metaphysical structure presented in *Finnegans Wake*. Furthermore, this demonstration will not be restricted solely to metaphysics. It should become apparent that our attempts to locate and reflect on the primary metaphysical notions embodied in Joyce's work will yield results of literary consequence, principally for evaluating how this metaphysical dimension affects the semantic and referential aspects of literary style.

Thus far I have attempted to beam the "light of philophosy" into metaphysical categories sufficiently translucent to illuminate at least some of the relevant literary obscurities in the initial reaches of the grand Joycean continuum. This cursory study of *Portrait* and *Ulysses* has attempted to introduce the importance of the metaphysical dimension in each of these works, as a way of directing readers toward a more adequate understanding of the limitless horizon of *Finnegans Wake*.

PART III
Wisdom and the Wake

The Conflict Between Style and Reality

From a philosophical perspective, the history of Joyce's prose style emerges as an increasingly penetrating inquiry into the relation between language and human consciousness of reality. The various metamorphoses in Joyce's style represent the need, instigated by the gradual recognition that consciousness apprehends its objects while in a state of flux, to merge literary language with the vast array of experiential content flowing through it. *Portrait* takes the first perhaps tentative steps, especially when Stephen Dedalus becomes more introspective about himself and his life with the written word; *Ulysses* advances confidently into many regions of self-awareness and the consciousness of others, and the *Wake* extends the limits of the flux so that it becomes virtually coincident with reality itself. As the culmination of Joyce's speculative vision, *Finnegans Wake* thus commands a pivotal view for appreciating the dominant force of the metaphysics of flux inscribed within the boundless reaches of this uniquely grand continuum.

Once it becomes apparent that a metaphysical vision of this magnitude has thoroughly permeated literary style, any truly comprehensive critical analysis must consider the effects of this vision. How then should such metaphysical inquiry and literary criticism be combined? If we begin by subjecting the metaphysics of the *Wake* to appropriate philosophical scrutiny, the results—suitably modified—should become relevant for developing a critical approach to the *Wake* based on principles which will allow the work to be more accessible as literature. In this chapter, we shall indicate areas in which we can formulate these principles and apply them to certain concrete problems in *Wake* exegesis. However, a comprehensive treatment detailing how the metaphysical dimension pertains to all phases of criticism relevant to a work of the *Wake*'s complexity is a project which lies beyond the scope of this study. It will be sufficient for now just to demonstrate that such a project is a worthy endeavor for the proper understanding of Joyce.

Of course, it is not merely that metaphysics is useful to literary criticism; the reverse is also true. It is a singular feature of the *Wake*'s language that the frequently radical metaphysics integrated into its exotic style forces the reader with certain metaphysical interests to consider alternatives to more established metaphysical positions, alternatives which might not have been conveyed in more conventionally academic expression. The comprehensive intellectual spectrum required for literary understanding of the *Wake* presupposes the recognition and appreciation of a wide variety of metaphysical possibilities. *Finnegans Wake* thus educates the student of metaphysics as it widens the horizons of the serious student of both literature and literary criticism. And given the interpretive direction of this study, it will not be idle to explore in this chapter some of these suggested metaphysical domains.

The format of this chapter resembles that of part I in that the four pairs of cardinal metaphysical notions—motion and rest, cause and effect, identity and difference, space and time—will guide us as we consider the final phase of the Joycean grand continuum. However, I have changed the order of exposition somewhat since the discussion of cause and effect now occurs immediately after motion and rest, for reasons that should become clear. While some of the metaphysical positions mentioned in this chapter have been introduced earlier, the discussion here focuses on their implications more sharply, both as metaphysics per se and as they relate to the literary understanding of the work.

Motion and Rest

That ideal reader who consents to travel the linguistic and experiential route of "Doublends Jined" cannot escape from the circuit of multiple meanings in the hope that the world can be released into language in a form other than that defined by the *Wake*'s metaphysics of flux. This reader is therefore compelled to accept the fact that whatever literary meanings are finally derived from the *Wake* depend, in an essential sense, on the metaphysical dimension which grounds these meanings. This conclusion becomes more important once we realize that amid the welter of puns and the bursts of boisterous humor, the maelstrom of *Finnegans Wake* revolves around a stark metaphysical premise which most philosophers would find difficult to defend. It was probably Heraclitus who first gave prominence to the notion that reality is perpetual flux. However, even in antiquity Heraclitus was known as "the dark one," and not just for the gnomic quality of his utterances but also for the paradoxes generated by their implications. The repercussions of the claim that everything is continually in flux are so drastic that, if pursued to their ultimate logical ends, they threaten the very possibility of intelligibly asserting this or any other claim as meaningful. One way of reaching this peculiarly self-destructive conclusion is to examine the concepts of motion and rest in light of their coexistence within universal flux.

Motion and rest are correlative terms—each depends on the other to establish its own identity, its own reality. But the language of the *Wake* would have it that rest, if understood as a metaphysical predicate of seemingly irreducible character, represents little more than an arbitrary ascription of limits. Although all avenues of human perception at some time or other yield the impression that things can be both recognized as instances of types and identified as particular things, these differences must eventually become submerged in the wake of universal flux. All such metaphysical distinctions are only temporary, their merely occasional mode of existence necessarily reflected in the fluctuating semantic quality of the language in which these distinctions are expressed.

This crucial consequence applies to every division of reality—to all types of being, however demarcated, and to all individual examples of all such types, regardless how manifestly diverse they may appear. This veritable dissolution of stability, especially for objects in space and time of fixed, or apparently fixed, character, is a dramatic consequence of the principle of unending flux. Less dramatic perhaps, but equally fundamental as a metaphysical repercussion, is the effect of this principle on distinctions within that one type of being of particular interest to students of Joyce—human consciousness. If, as seems perfectly reasonable, consciousness can be divided into waking experience and dreaming, then the former can be typified as consciousness in which stability and rest predominate, where the objects of consciousness are normally discerned with clearly definable limits. Here it is obvious that a gravestone is not the same as a young lady bathing on the beach. Dream consciousness, on the other hand, may be characterized by the opposite in that it is inhabited primarily by shapes and forms swirling through many different identities. Roughly put, motion could be said to function with respect to the nature of dream consciousness approximately as stasis relates to the structure of waking consciousness.

But even the possibility of drawing such a superfically apt distinction vanishes if the stability proper to waking consciousness is, in point of metaphysical fact, no more stable than the elusive motion proper to dreaming. To be awake and to be asleep become indistinguishable if no standard—itself impervious to restless motion—is available whereby the distinction can be determined. And the *Wake* assures us that no such standard exists.

This destruction of differences unsettles our sense of the real in many respects. But to reject it or the premise from which it originates may be premature. For if we trust the *Wake*'s guiding principle, then the merging of dreaming and waking may turn out to be metaphysically instructive. The more the flowing properties of dream consciousness can be insinuated into the static nature of waking consciousness, the greater the possibility that the structure of reality will be known as it really is. If this process of constructive destruction requires periodic forays into the restless phenomena of dreams, then so be it. Since in the final analysis all limits are arbitrary, they must somehow be broken down into the appropriate currents of flux. Nevertheless, the suspicion still lingers that even these vigorously stated currents of flux must retain some identifying definition, some species of individuating form. And if a certain degree or type of form is somehow to be preserved, then perpetual and universal flux cannot by itself fulfill the demands of coherent metaphysical thought.

In the world of flux, the limits implied by traditional conceptions of language must also be set aside. And the repercussions here are even more drastic, even more dire. In part I, the introductory analysis of *Wake* language appealed to the well-known philosophical distinction between meaning and reference by way of contrast to the *Wake*'s account of how words work. Now as soon as the referential function of the *Wake*'s language must incorporate the fact that all entities referred to are continually changing, it will then follow that a linguistic element appearing to refer to one entity may also be referring concurrently to another entity. In fact, if everything is in flux, then there is no reason why a reference seemingly to one particular thing cannot be taken as referring to every other thing as well. Therefore, the meaning ascribed to a given utterance in the *Wake* must take into account this peculiar floating referential quality. For the continual motion of all referents in the *Wake* establishes, in parallel fashion, the possibility—if not the actuality—of unlimited meanings whenever language enters into relation with the flux of beings as objects of reference.

Here again, the introduction of motion, in particular semantic motion as derived from referential motion, contributes to an increased awareness of the presence of perpetual flux. Whatever has heretofore limited linguistic meanings no longer exercises this power; language thus assumes a perspective on totality as comprehensive as totality existing in its own right, apart from language. Just as the identity of a given referent may come to include all that which is seemingly other than that referent, so the meaning of any sentence in the *Wake* is susceptible to virtually unlimited expansion.

But a question analogous in scope to the one raised about entities also arises here, concerning discourse about entities. For if the meaning assigned to the *Wake* as a whole is in a flux of range and intensity equivalent to all the narrative of the *Wake* is about, then how can the *Wake* be said to have *any* meaning? To assert, as critics are naturally required to do, that the *Wake* (or any part of the *Wake*) means A, B, C . . . up to some finite point is still to limit the meaning of a referentially limitless whole, even if the serial order of meanings is of considerable length and complexity. But once the metaphysics of *Finnegans Wake* expands its purely linguistic phase into seemingly boundless dimensions, how can any critical analysis of the *Wake*, whether aimed at a part or the whole, necessarily be anything other than an exercise in arbitrarily restricted interpretation? Perhaps the apparently unavoidable tension between what the *Wake*'s critic wants to be able to say and what the *Wake* allows to be said is one reason, metaphysical in character but nonetheless quite real, why critical discourse about the *Wake* is so difficult. It seems that critics must at some point justify their activity by grappling with those metaphysical implications of the *Wake* which would deny them the very possibility of such interpretive discussion. And as we shall see, the difficulties raised by these implications and their underlying principles may be easily demonstrated.

Cause and Effect

There are at least two distinct contexts in which the *Wake* dislocates the customary relationship linking cause and effect. The first is within the world of the *Wake* itself. There we discover that the priority of cause to effect no longer holds. As a result, events—or, perhaps less misleadingly, processes—are totally bereft of causal order. Events merely occur, without rhyme, reason, or rhythm. But if causality of any sort is lacking in the natural order, then we should not be surprised by anything that happens in the narrative proper. Thus the future may never resemble the past, given that the customary priority of cause to effect may always be reversed. And once cause *A* and effect *B* may become effect *A* and cause *B*, then it becomes virtually impossible to distinguish any sense of priority—indeed, any difference at all—between them.

As an important corollary, we should repeat that once causal priority ceases to exist, then if the difference between "past" and "future" time is determined primarily by the priority of cause to effect, then this difference disappears; time collapses into an undifferentiated continual present. The virtual disappearance of causal and temporal order in turn has important implications for the literary comprehension of the *Wake*. For any critical observations based on the implicit understanding that a given character or event can be causally related to another character or event will lack metaphysical ground. Again, the possibility of criticism would seem to be negated by the implications flowing from the *Wake*'s own metaphysical principles.

The second context of unhinged causality is external to the world of the *Wake* in that it concerns the relation between that world and the reader who exists, at least in some respects, in a world far different in metaphysical structure. At the point where the reader of the *Wake* begins to understand language and nonlinguistic reality as mirror images of one another, we must examine the relation between them in order to preserve the sense of difference between, say, an actual river and the word "river," a linguistic token for representing that particular fluid entity. This relation may be approached by examining the potentially causal agency existing between certain conventions proper to language as a medium of representation and nonlinguistic reality as such. More specifically, let us attempt to determine the principal metaphysical effects felt by a reader existing in the world outside of the *Wake* and engaged at the same time in trying to understand *Wake* language in relation to that world.

In the chapter called "The Flux of Language," we examined how the conventions of spelling, grammar, and syntax have been extensively altered in order to accommodate the grand scope of the *Wake*'s metaphysical vision of flux. The pertinent question now is whether these conventions, fixed and thus not subject to analysis when customarily applied, have significant metaphysical repercussions. Do these conventions contain—and conceal—metaphysical principles? Do they somehow cause the reader to experience the reality thus represented linguistically in certain invariable ways just by their presence on the printed page? If so, then these currently concealed factors may be thrust into the open and scrutinized once these conventions have been replaced by seemingly idiosyncratic literary devices. Furthermore, the possibility that linguistic conventions themselves have a causal effect on our perception and our account of reality will eventually force us to question how, in general, language should be situated within a comprehensive world view. Are we philosophically educated by our discourse *about* the world as much (indeed, perhaps even more so) as we are by our perceptual and reflective experience *in* and *of* the world? The *Wake* implies that this possibility is quite real, with ramifications perhaps as disturbing as they are intriguing, at least for all those who rest content in some sort of stability external to the perpetual flux of the *Wake*.

It would doubtless be difficult to measure accurately the extent to which the conventions of written language have contributed, if at all, to our unreflective sense of the rhythms of reality. But it is clear that the systematic metaphysical vision of the *Wake* is intended in part to compensate for this potential shortsightedness. Another related aspect of this compensation is the introduction of languages other than English into the *Wake*. Furthermore, even that ideal reader who has mastered a number of languages is compelled to read and understand all these languages *simultaneously*. In one sense, of course, this confluence of linguistic streams may simply compound the distortions found in any one language. After all, if every natural language contains some metaphysical preconceptions, then a mere juxtaposition of such one-sided perspectives will hardly bring about a more rounded view of the common reality which these languages were created to describe.

But there is another possibility, one more positive and instructive metaphysically. For it is also conceivable that the relevant structural features of all the languages found in the *Wake* have torn loose from their traditional conceptual and metaphysical moorings. The *Wake* then replaces these now rootless languages with a linguistic system carefully grounded in an ordered metaphysical position. As a result, the complexity of language in the *Wake* induces us to situate ourselves somehow within that unique linguistic world view. And the effort to understand this complexity could yield insight into the character of reality of that world—the "real" world—existing outside the linguistic parameters described by the *Wake*'s own universe.

The philosophical enterprise itself will be an important offshoot of this confrontation. As I have attempted to show, traditional philosophical discourse establishes its uniqueness by manifesting a certain universality of scope. But in light of the causal efficacy attributed by the *Wake* to language itself, the type of language eventually selected to represent reality from the philosophical standpoint becomes a matter of considerable importance. Thus, *how* philosophical language says what it says is tantamount to *what* that language says. For example, the more reality is characterized by swirling flux, the more the customarily abstract and experientially neutral terminology of technical philosophy will tend to deflect the real immediacy of that flux. In fact, the very attempt to elicit any form of universal philosophical expression risks distorting the vibrancy of texture present in whatever these expressions are intended to represent. This risk becomes proportionately high if the uniqueness of each entity in the referential range of language is defined in terms of continual flux, the entity constantly shifting in and through the myriad forms which this mode of reality must assume.

Therefore, when choosing the most apposite philosophical vocabulary, especially for expressing a metaphysical picture of reality, we should bear in mind the relation between the content of experience and the analogical kinship found in the linguistic representations of experience. We must take into account not just what the terms mean and the fact that language is capable of referring to things or events, but also how the terms have been elicited from the total flux of experience and the immensely varied and rich store of language available to describe that experience. For an integral element of both the semantic and referential functions of philosophical discourse will now be the extent to which these functions evoke *the actual experience* of the reality they attempt to embody. With its frequently uncanny merger of flux-metaphysics and fluid puns, the *Wake* has vividly demonstrated this potential connection between terminological medium and philosophical message. The point here is not that future metaphysicians must cut their sapiential teeth on Joycean prose. But what should perhaps be taken into account is the possibility that language is sufficiently supple to produce a considerable degree of proximity between reality as conceptualized and those terms which, through an interplay of sound and sense, bring the student of metaphysics closer to the feel of reality as actually experienced.

Identity and Difference

Securing the most appropriate language for philosophical discourse is one problem whose implications effectively bridge the metaphysical gap separating cause and effect from identity and difference. Philosophy's inherent drive toward universality necessarily forces a philosophical term or proposition to represent identity over difference—that is, the identical features present in entities or properties or events differing in some respects from one another. But language can achieve this goal only if, as a matter of metaphysical fact, its referential function is substantiated by real objects to which one can refer, and which can be distinguished as "identical" and "different." Yet we have seen that no such objects can exist, at least when the full weight of the *Wake*'s metaphysics has been brought to bear on their apparently stable mode of reality.

Perhaps the most dramatic consequences of the *Wake*'s metaphysics of flux become evident under this rubric of identity and difference. For perpetual motion ultimately implies that there can be no lasting distinctions accounting for difference, and no criteria for determining identity. There is no individuation of one thing from another, or of one type from another—HCE and ALP are two moments awash in the same ever-flowing stream, and the river Liffey is as much an artifact as the letter is natural, appearances to the contrary notwithstanding. There is no real distinction between universal and particular, or between entity and process. All particular things are universals, all entities are processes. Opposites no longer play into and from one another in symmetrical harmony—motion and rest are two names for the same state (or, equivalently, the same name for two states only apparently different but, in fact, metaphysically indistinguishable). There is no possibility of personal identity, of a particular instance of consciousness being this person and not that person (or, indeed, that thing). There are no distinct psychological functions—thus, for example, memory and imagination become equivalent in both scope and detail. What is remembered as having been and what is imagined as what might have been now merge. This catalogue of vanishing differences could continue indefinitely.

These consequences obviously run counter to our commonsense grasp of reality. Surely the fact that at least some differences and identities *appear to be fixed* must be taken into account in conjunction with the metaphysical claim that such differentiation is only a superficial arrangement of basically formless and chaotic flux. Let us consider in more detail the apparent need for preserving identity and difference in that metaphysical region in which the reality of language and all types of nonlinguistic reality become tangent to one another. This will establish a limited context for situating the primary literary implications of the *Wake*'s metaphysics.

The *Wake* asserts that when an entity enters language, it cannot remain metaphysically identical to itself—it becomes subject, as referent, to all differentiations of meaning generated by the ascription of language to that entity. Thus the typical *Wake* pun is referentially opaque—it can, indeed must, be read as referring to two (or many) different entities at the same time. These entities may be quite distinct from one another, at least with respect to a non-*Wake* mode of perception. They may be particulars (existing at various historical times) types, or abstractions. But all possible referents, regardless of any apparent differences, must be included within the denotative scope of each appropriately punning word, with the correlative semantic range of these words possessing an equivalently expanding scope.

It is not difficult to see how a distinctively linguistic version of the problematic repercussion of endless flux described above will arise. In order to emphasize the radical character of this aspect of the flux, we shall deploy the meaning/reference distinction in a broad enough framework to accommodate the demands placed on language by the *Wake*'s metaphysical principles. Assume therefore that each referent in a *Wake* pun has what might be called a "zone of meaning." The semantic limits of each zone will then depend on the number of referents generated by that pun. As the number of referents increases, so will the number of potential semantic elements constituting the zone of meaning. The greater the number of these elements, the more complex becomes the semantic range of each word, and the more difficult it is to determine any one meaning common to all the referential elements of that zone. When the number of referents is indefinitely large, any attempt to determine a corresponding meaning becomes, at best, a selective gathering of referential elements and the resultant prescribed meanings. Thus, in pushing to the limits the relation between language and what language must do in order to abide by the dictates of the *Wake*'s metaphysics, we strain to the utmost the possibility of preserving significance within any part of the work and to the work as a whole.

At this point, we must set up some interpretive limits. In order to retain the possibility that meaning can be ascribed to a complex literary work, let us attempt to distinguish between what might be called the primary and the secondary referents of a given *Wake* word. Consider, for example, the word "commodious." It seems clear that the primary referent of this word is a certain spatial dimension. Secondary referents include the Roman emperor Commodus and a species of chamber pot. There are doubtless other referents as well, but these three will serve to illustrate the procedure intended. Now is there any discernible relation between the primary and the secondary referents of this word? Are they joined together by simple and discrete conjunction or by a flux-like oscillation during which there remains some form of identity? And even if this question could be answered, the nature of the referential connection (or lack of one) would remain independent of the purely semantic relation existing between a type of space, a Roman emperor, and a hygenic vessel. On the assumption that a meaning relation does exist between and among the various referents of a given pun, then apparently some criterion should determine which meanings will be primary to the central narrative flow and which will be secondary. For without such a criterion, it becomes impossible to preserve the difference between and among all the various potential meanings of each word. Can such a criterion be derived from within the roomy world of the *Wake?*

In a word, no. At least, not without serious inconsistency with its fundamental metaphysical principles. Thus the interpretive strategy just sketched turns out to be little more than a counsel of expediency. For if there were such a standard, it would have to remain somehow apart from the flux in order to exhibit the requisite identity for stipulating the difference between primary and secondary referents. But if it were apart from the flux, then it would no longer be in contact with the driving agency moving the world of the *Wake*—i.e., perpetually restless and formless flux. After all, universal flux by definition means that nothing lies outside its bounds. Yet surely there must be some such mode of existence in which one referent can be called primary and another secondary, thus preserving the possibility of critically ranking the various meanings associated with these referents. Consequently, it appears that the critic must run directly against the metaphysical currents of the *Wake* simply to be in a position to say anything at all about the work.

This seemingly fruitful approach for establishing the possibility of meaning in the *Wake* has thus proved abortive, another victim of the onslaught of the flux. As a result, we can assert that the relation between language and nonlinguistic reality becomes difficult, if not impossible, to discern. And yet this particular repercussion, so fundamentally opposed to sound metaphysical sense, can from the critic's point of view be put to good use. For the very elusiveness of this relation carries with it suggestions which, properly formulated, point the way toward solutions of a sort to several vexing issues in *Wake* interpretation. We shall address these problems and attempt to answer them from the vantage point just reached.

Since personal identity is, at best, only a temporary means of specification in the *Wake*, there can be no real distinction between a first- and third-person account of events, between an individual consciousness voicing what is actually being experienced by that consciousness and an external observer reporting what is happening at a distance from that observer. Furthermore, the metaphysical groundlessness of this distinction necessitates the virtual disappearance of any distance between the nameless narrator of the *Wake* and the audience. The extent to which a reader of the *Wake* participates in the world begotten by that work is the extent to which that reader both is defined by and defines the limits of that world. If we enter the *Wake*, then we implicitly agree to interpret the significance of that world by allowing its metaphysics to structure our sense of reality and our critical apprehension of the elements which constitute that structure.

It follows, one may argue, that all the critical concern for identifying the narrator of *Finnegans Wake* rests on not taking the implications of the *Wake*'s metaphysics to their ultimate conclusions. Since there is no real difference between narrator and what is narrated, the individual reader narrates the events of the *Wake* as much as do the *Wake*'s mysterious dreamer, HCE, ALP, their various transmogrifications, etc. To isolate a narrator solely from *within* the *Wake* and then to stand off apart from that narrator while trying to divine his or her identity is, implicitly, to situate the *Wake* in a metaphysical and literary vacuum, divorcing its radically esoteric character from the comfortable domesticity of our commonsense hold on the real. It is, in fact, to preserve a difference—between the reality of the reader and the reality described in the *Wake*—when there can be only an undifferentiated identity—the reader and the words of the *Wake* fusing into a whole, its dimensions dictated by the reader's knowledge when inhabiting those words.

But even the most erudite and imaginative reader of the *Wake* can know only so much. Even this ideal reader will doubtless fall short in the arena of naked knowledge required for full mastery of the *Wake*'s seemingly limitless subtleties. Who then will serve as the omniscient Joycean oracle? Anthony Burgess has answered this question by contending that the *Wake* would not present a semantic puzzle for anyone who brought to the work as much as Joyce did when he wrote it. In short, the meaning of the *Wake* as a whole is identical to what its author indended it to mean.

Yet what if the knowledge of the author could somehow be reproduced—will it follow that the semantic scope of the *Wake* would be stabilized? Surely not. For whatever Joyce himself could have identified as the referents of a given pun would be differentiated by that identification and thus become fixed. As fixed, however, their mode of reality would then conflict with what the *Wake* has declared to be the metaphysically proper mode of reality of all things. Thus we must infer that the language of the *Wake* should be understood so that it means even *more* than what was consciously, or even unconsciously, intended by its author. How, for example, are we to identify the referents and determine the meaning of a word like "chaosmos"? If Joyce envisioned a neologism formed by the different words "cosmos" and "chaos," then the semantic and referential polarity of these two opposites must become conjoined into a new identity, one which certainly defies the ascription of either static or fluid predicates. But what third alternative is there, given that motion and rest are jointly exhaustive categories? That there could be a third meaning depends upon realizing an insight into the reality of the flux which surely transcends even the limitless reaches of the Joycean imagination.

One may or may not rest content with answers such as these to what have become almost classical issues in *Wake* exegesis. But even if these answers are persuasive, there are other effects, more disturbing than illuminating, following upon the principles just applied to these issues. For it seems inevitable that any of the available attempts to establish some form of identity, either with respect to entities or to language about entities, must fail by virtue of the unlimited force of the *Wake*'s metaphysical flux. In fact, the very possibility of a difference between entities as such and language about entities begins to fade in the face of that flux. Even if a referent or set of referents, however complex, could be isolated and identified as proper to a given *Wake* word, the universal flux demands that the language referring to these entities cannot maintain a mode of existence as self-contained and self-identical phenomenon. As a result, language can never move beyond itself to a domain of referred entities for the simple but metaphysically necessary reason that nothing exhibits the stability and self-identity required so that anything linguistic can be predicated of anything existing in an extralinguistic frame of reference.

The *Wake*'s metaphysics thus culminates in a telling and exquisitely paradoxical self-referential effect, one akin to the snake swallowing its tail until there is no tail left to be swallowed—and no snake either. For if what is said in the *Wake* about language and the relation between language and extralinguistic reality refers to the *Wake* itself, then *Finnegans Wake* as a literary entity existing within the world it describes becomes impossible to talk about. To talk about something presupposes at least the implicit acceptance of a difference between language as a medium of expression and whatever may be the intended object. Here again, however, we cannot permit this seemingly incontrovertible difference, being inconsistent with the universality of the *Wake*'s grounding metaphysics. But how then can the *Wake* establish itself as a literary vehicle constituted, in one essential phase of its structure, as a metaphysical system when by the very strength of that system it cannot retain a mode of existence distinct from anything else existing within that system? This question depends for its critical relevance on our locating the *Wake*'s metaphysics squarely within the confines of a very literal, precisely logical framework. But without such a close reading, the uniquely radical character of that metaphysics cannot be properly appreciated. From this perspective, the *Wake* challenges us to reconcile its seemingly skewed metaphysical vision with the demands of logic, demands which, by tradition and the apparent nature of reason itself, control our understanding of what is, is not, and can be meaningful discourse.

Space and Time

The seemingly stable difference between language and everything other than language has been rendered groundless by the metaphysical implications of perpetual motion, especially as exemplified through the resulting formlessness of entities within the spatio-temporal world. This particular repercussion, so drastically at odds with our customary sense of the real, epitomizes the need to scrutinize all the more closely the *Wake*'s most fundamental principles. The pressure mounts to find some persuasive and consistent way to halt the *Wake*'s rampaging flux. For even space and time themselves suffer the same self-destructive consequences, quite apart from the entities or events existing or transpiring within spatio-temporal limits. These consequences should also be traced out in order to bring the full brunt of the flux into the open in all relevant perspectives. And in the process, we may discern how to interpret these consequences in such a way as to produce literary and philosophical effects as tentative conclusions for this survey of the nature and influence of metaphysics in *Finnegans Wake*.

Let us review briefly the relevant properties of time as discussed in part I. Traditional metaphysical accounts of time have depended heavily on the apparent credibility of such distinctions as "before" and "after," and on the demarcations of time into past, present, future. As we have seen, however, the narrative structure of the *Wake* has established time as one immense all-enveloping circle endlessly repeating itself. Now a circle is an instance of a geometrical totality. But if time is then understood as a totality defined by circularity, how can "before" and "after" be meaningful designations? All before and after relations become relative, since precisely the same circle incorporating all such relations can be generated in both clockwise and counterclockwise directions. The temporal content of a given before/after relation thus seems to depend solely on the fiat of the reader.

One might object that the narrative of the *Wake* moves in only one rotary direction, a textual fact presumably independent of any reader's consciousness. But even if this one-direction rotary motion is retained for the *Wake*'s cycle of events, the same quality of undifferentiatedness results. The pagination of the *Wake* goes from 3 to 628. But the circular nature of narrative temporality is such that although what happens on page 628 comes *after* what happens on page 3, once the second revolution of the narrative as a whole begins, the events of page 628 come *before* those on page 3. The upshot is that each member of a specific pair of events can be ordered both as "before" and as "after" the other member. As a result, any literary assessment based on the apparent temporal succession of events within one traversal of the circular narrative may have to be altered, in detail or in essence, once such temporal successions are reversed (as indeed they always could be).

Now once there is no objectively measurable before and after, then there can be no real difference between the past and the present, or between the present and the future. If we then assume that temporality nonetheless maintains a vestige of reality, it becomes unavoidably reduced to something like a simultaneous present. But if time as such is nothing but simultaneity, then how can distinguishable events happen *in* time? A circular temporality happens all at once, so to speak, without the possibility of duration—the actual passing of time—generating temporal difference as a factor capable of distinguishing one event from another. In fact, how can time as a continuous present be asserted to possess any shape whatsoever, be it cyclical, linear, or following any other configuration?

The collapse of time into an undifferentiated present is mirrored by a similar collapse of space into an unbounded place. The demise of space in the *Wake* is, however, presented in a more inferentially complex mode than that of time. The inferences are nonetheless visible as implications following upon the *Wake*'s metaphysical principles.

The *Wake* contends that all entities are actually in the process of becoming something other than themselves, especially as they assume shape and form in language. It will follow then that there can be no real spatial distance between distinguishably different entities for the simple reason that there is no metaphysical ground for such distance. In short, there can be no spatial "between" because all existing things are always changing, always taking up whatever room may appear to exist between this and that apparently distinct entity.

A different but related linguistic path leads to the same rather cramped conclusion. As the number of referents for each *Wake* word increases, the number of entities referred to increases commensurately. We have already attempted to show that each word is capable of entering into transformations which ultimately will denote the referential totality of the *Wake*'s linguistic world. Thus the limits of space as entailed by the referential status of the *Wake*'s entities are also transformed into a dimension limited only by totality—in effect, without limits whatsoever. Space in the *Wake* cannot be demarcated into regions, areas, or coordinates, because there is nothing against which any standard of measurement, any source of limitation, can be set.

This remarkable consequence is generated by the unique drive toward totality incorporated within the referential function of the *Wake*'s language coupled with the virtual annihilation of any mode of difference between and among entities. Although the phrasing of the point may sound quixotic, there is a very real sense in which the world of the *Wake* is a place where somewhere is anywhere and everywhere is nowhere. All narrative events are thus not only concurrent in an everlastingly undifferentiated present, they are also omnipresent in a spatially unlimited place. But how can such sprawling universality be possible? Here again, the pressure of a commonsense grasp on reality becomes palpably, if not urgently, present. For an entity or event without spatial parameters of some sort verges on metaphysical invisibility; it is not discernible as *an* event or *an* entity somehow distinct from other events and entities. Once more, we discover conflict between the finely articulated quality of events happening in the *Wake* and the metaphysics grounding the reality of those events, a metaphysics which can permit such articulation only in the most evanescent sense.

The dissolution of differentiated space is an indirect repercussion of the referential function of the *Wake*'s language. And the combined collapse of space-time eventually results in the virtual dissolution of two additional properties traditionally associated with a metaphysical understanding of language. The first is truth. According to one theory, still held in some form by many philosophers, truth may be represented as a correspondence between a sentence and a state of affairs. Thus the sentence "*Finnegans Wake* is set in Dublin" is true if that sentence corresponds to that state of affairs in which, as a matter of fact, *Finnegans Wake* is set in Dublin. But notice that if it has become impossible to discern the limits of a state of affairs, then it also becomes impossible to determine whether a given sentence does or does not correspond to that now unlimited moment of flux. Such is the destiny of truth in the *Wake* that it becomes indistinguishable from "untruth," to use the *Wake*'s own apt locution. Thus, truth no longer commands language as it once did because the metaphysical conditions requisite for distinguishing between something true and something false no longer obtain. However the notion of truth may be analyzed, as long as the resulting theoretical representation includes a linguistic element construed in a mode of existence distinct from that of its referents, the same self-destructive repercussion for truth will result. The *Wake*'s flux brooks no such distinctions.

The second property, the relation between language and the axioms of logic, leads the student of Joycean metaphysics to the very limits of intelligibility. It has already been noted how an ingenious (and tireless) reader could multiply the number of meanings of every word in the *Wake* to an exponent of almost limitless magnitude. If, however, each word can generate such a raft of significance, then this same reader can, in more diabolically perverse moments, construe these meanings as sentences which may—and perhaps in some cases must—contradict one another.

Now according to one interpretation in contemporary philosophy of logic, a contradiction is a sentence lacking significance by virtue of the self-destructive conflict contained within the form of the utterance as such. The logician P. F. Strawson tells us that "contradicting oneself is like writing something down and then erasing it, or putting a line through it. A contradiction cancels itself and leaves nothing."[1] Thus the conjunction of sentences "*Finnegans Wake* is about HCE" and "*Finnegans Wake* is not about HCE" forms a self-contradictory assertion, one from which it is impossible to tell anything, much less what *Finnegans Wake* is about.

It becomes evident upon reflection that even the language of literature must obey the principle of contradiction, at least to a certain degree. Try, for example, to imagine a perversely quixotic literary work composed of nothing but contradictions; or, perhaps less unorthodox, a work in which certain descriptive accounts contained periodic contradictions. What could such a work express? As we have seen, the metaphysical principles of the *Wake* allow, if not demand, that the meaning of its language should be so multiform that contradictions will inevitably result. Therefore, once we heed the formal self-destruction of language entailed by these contradictions, then all *Wake* language governed by this implicit denial of the legitimacy of contradiction becomes devoid of significance and reduced to meaninglessness. Nevertheless, the very language asserting the questionable ultimacy of the principle of contradiction is, or at least appears to be, meaningful, at least on the immediate level. The *Wake* thus has the paradoxical character of both implicitly and explicitly denying the principle of contradiction at the same time that it depends on that very principle as a necessary prerequisite for meaningfully positing thus ultraradical position.

This paradox may be interpreted in at least two senses. The first is primarily negative, although not without its own instructive insight in terms of a philosophical understanding of the general contours of the *Wake*'s metaphysics. For the above argument suggests that the very attempt to erect principles of interpretation appropriate for the *Wake* becomes problematic at best, since these principles will depend, both in their formulation and in their application, on contradiction and all the other logical axioms which the *Wake* has explicitly questioned, if not denied. The metaphysics of the *Wake,* and by implication the literary substance of the work as a whole, would thus be skewed if we attempted to make it meaningful according to the principles of logic. And since in our non-*Wake* moments we seem necessarily beholden to the demands of formal logic, this interpretive perspective offers little useful guidance toward understanding the full philosophical import of an apparently very illogical literary work.

The other sense is more positive; indeed it is pregnant with intriguing and somewhat unusual philosophical possibilities. Consider the fact that language has been traditionally thought to be controlled by the formal principles of logic. However, this understanding may, in the wake of the *Wake,* become subservient to the more palpable reality of language occurring in a historical, temporally flowing setting. In fact, the principle of contradiction itself may have derived its sacrosanct status by way of an abstraction—perhaps a distorting abstraction—from the cosmic totality of space-time understood in a more fluid metaphysical context such as that presented in part by the *Wake*.

This perceptively daring possibility, originating from reflection on the purely formal linguistic function of contradiction, ramifies into all aspects of language and, ultimately, into all aspects of experience. For if the temporality underlying the principle of contradiction is indeed shown to be only a hypothetical abstraction, then perhaps it is possible that things should be perceived in a temporal framework other than what has been traditionally understood as essential. In this case, the *Wake*'s unearthing of the assumptions about space and time latent in the origin and development of all natural languages points the way toward a revamped experience of space and time. We may begin to realize this end by analyzing the notion that language can somehow "refer" to something other than itself, the analysis being especially concerned with the essentially embedded space-time structure present in the process of referring. Therefore, if space-time is indeed ingrained "in" language, then it will follow that the specification of the abstract properties pertaining to reference as a purely linguistic concept must also include the specification of the spatio-temporal properties implicit in the process of referring. For the *Wake* has taught us in a variety of ways that reference can no longer be understood as a linguistic notion neutral to metaphysical considerations.

The positive direction for interpreting the *Wake*'s paradoxical self-referential aspects can be extended even further. Let us briefly consider two possibilities. First, the more we know about the *Wake*'s "dream language," the greater the number of perspectives will be opened on a more diversified and comprehensive apprehension of space-time as such. One especially relevant area of application concerns a more adequate solution to the classic metaphysical problem of individuating entities from one another, a problem which may finally depend on a much more complex understanding of space-time than provided by most traditional accounts. This solution may be funded, at least in part, by spatio-temporal considerations present in the language of *Finnegans Wake,* especially in that significant and mysterious form of consciousness in which we sleep and dream.

Second, it seems reasonable to assume that language has certain metaphysical presuppositions which can be brought to light for critical examination. These presuppositions may or may not be subject to distortions affecting the nature of reality as it appears in its linguistic transcriptions. Assume that such distortion is present in all natural languages. We may then wonder to what extent language must necessarily remain wholly natural. For it is possible that a thoughtful confluence of these different tongues, blended into a new if somewhat unfamiliar unity, could somehow reduce the distorting scope of these presuppositions. Furthermore, if the philosophical enterprise as one vital instance of linguistic activity requires the formulation and expression of abstract language—as it apparently does—then the more these abstractions are forged from meanings drawn from the totality of these languages, the more likely that these abstractions will approximate the "true" character of reality. The *Wake* makes us *feel* language in new and frequently disconcerting ways. Perhaps these textures will serve to initiate the restoration of a sense of the whole which has been gradually lost due to the continually increasing pressure of an overly rigidified and static metaphysics, both as expressly developed in the history of philosophy and as implicitly reflected in the history of literature.

As *Finnegans Wake* approaches the climactic moments of its narrative cycle, ALP is in the process of being transformed into a river, perhaps all rivers—indeed, perhaps into the water which Thales, the first philosopher, contended was the principle of all reality. A river receives its sustenance from raindrops falling from the heavens, and for ALP the heavens themselves become an integral part of this liquid metamorphosis even when the sky is blue and moisture is absent from its limitless reaches. The she-river sings that the heavens are "my great blue bedroom, the air so quiet, scarce a cloud" (627.9). After hundreds of pages of crabbed and convoluted prose, the lilting rhythms and precise imagery of this brief sentence burst forth, an especially prominent exemplar of lyrical splendor. We do not often see this particular aspect of Joyce's art in the *Wake,* but its presence here illustrates the fact that Joyce had not lost the capacity to fashion delicately wrought prose when the narrative situation and mood required such language. I have left this and other manifest literary qualities in these works all but untouched, concentrating instead on the philosophical character of Joyce's prose. Joycean language represents a neatly crafted congruence of literature and philosophy, so much so that a commentary devoted the more philosophical aspects of Joyce's work cannot help but shed light on its literary qualities. In fact, my own conviction is that the "light of philophosy" illuminates not just *Finnegans Wake,* not just *Portrait* and *Ulysses* seen in conjunction with the *Wake,* but the very limits of literary language itself as these limits run tangent to philosophical principles and notions developed in a metaphysical setting. Once Joyce is read and studied with an appropriately broad intellectual background and a sympathetic diversity of approach, the sometimes jostling interplay between the literary and the philosophical in his work raises essential metaphysical questions as well as important literary ones. Thus the attempt to orient ourselves with what the *Wake* says about reality produces unavoidable tensions between the flowing metaphysical shapes looming in the *Wake*'s world and what we feel certain—perhaps without justification—are indissoluble forms of fixedness. These tensions are manifested in a series of paradoxical depictions of reality so vividly delineated and forcefully expressed that they inevitably cause the student of the *Wake* (and, to a lesser degree, of *Portrait* and *Ulysses*) to think through these paradoxes until some measure of resolution is attained.

In this regard, the *Wake*'s position on the principle of contradiction in particular and logical axioms in general may serve as one especially instructive point of departure. The *Wake* implies that there exists a level of reality of such primordial character that it renders contradiction, the ultimate ordering principle of rational discourse, at best derivative and at worst distorting. A contemporary of Joyce's also had thoughts on these matters: "The principle of contradiction and the principle of identity are presupposed as self-evident without questioning whether something ultimate is present along with these principles." In another work, the same thinker asserts that the peculiarly Aristotelian formulation of contradiction must be questioned to determine "what this principle presupposes" in order to grasp more fully how it became instituted as "a regulative principle of thinking."[2] The speaker of these thoughts—the philosopher Martin Heidegger (1889–1976). Could this intriguing similarity between Heidegger's intensely sombre thought and Joyce's rollicking impressions mean that we are entitled to place Joyce's work, especially *Finnegans Wake,* in apposition to other significant figures of twentieth-century philosophical speculation?[3]

In the final chapter, we shall highlight a series of provocative links between the metaphysical structure of *Finnegans Wake* and the more self-consciously abstract positions of two pivotal yet diverse representatives of contemporary philosophy. Whether knowingly or otherwise, Joyce touched upon a number of contemporary lines of thought, with the result that the seemingly wrongheaded quality of his underlying principles may not be quite so illogical after all. If a significant portion of the theoretical aspects of Joyce's vision is shared by several of his more prosaic philosophical counterparts, then perhaps the purely literary aspects of Joyce's work will, under scrutiny, also seem less idiosyncratic and more meaningful to the reader who approaches his work as literature. This introductory survey of Joyce's metaphysics will then have established a set of guidelines capable of being adapted to a more detailed exercise in Joycean literary criticism.

Joycean Language and Contemporary Philosophy

This chapter attempts to substantiate the argument that the metaphysics of *Finnegans Wake* is relevant to reality as we understand it. I will follow a roundabout route. In the last chapter, I juxtaposed the *Wake*'s position on the derivative status of the principle of contradiction against several assertions by the philosopher Martin Heidegger. In these assertions, Heidegger maintained an approach as daring as Joyce's toward assessing the metaphysical import of that principle. This doctrinal parallelism suggests that Joyce and Heidegger, although outwardly occupying very different humanistic worlds, may not be so far apart in at least one crucial respect. It would be an instructive, if protracted, exercise to explore the extent to which Joyce and Heidegger share other philosophical concerns. However, I have chosen two other philosophers to serve this purpose—Ludwig Wittgenstein (1889–1953) and Edmund Husserl (1859–1938). Both contemporaries of Joyce, Wittgenstein and Husserl are vanguard figures in two leading areas of modern philosophy—ordinary language philosophy and phenomenology.

These two disciplines are, in a number of respects, at ideological odds; yet for our purposes, this tension can be used to create a more diversified arena within which to exhibit the relevance of the Joycean metaphysics. As we shall see, that metaphysics is sufficiently broad to touch on a number of intriguing analyses advanced by both these positions. And the similarities and differences arising from each confrontation will indicate how far the *Wake's* metaphysical vision coheres with those of two avowedly philosophical contemporaries.

Wittgenstein and Joyce

Ludwig Wittgenstein spent the philosophical part of his life battling with the vagaries of language, and his importance as a thinker lies in the fact that even when his conclusions are incomplete, his technique and sensitivity to linguistic nuance often illuminate areas of linguistic activity which previously were not recognized as problematic. The feature of this thought relevant here is the shift found in his later work toward understanding language as constituted by an indefinitely large number of what Wittgenstein called "language-games." However, in order to set in relief some of the most important differences in the two ways Wittgenstein approached language, I have provided an abstract of his earlier thought, as represented by his now classic work, the *Tractatus Logico-Philosophicus* (1921).

For the young Wittgenstein, "The world is all that is the case."[1] The term "case" here means "the totality of facts, not of things" (1.1). What is a fact? It is "the existence of states of affairs" (2). And here language makes its appearance, for in stocking his universe with facts rather than with things, Wittgenstein needs something with which to construct facts—thus, "We picture facts to ourselves" (2.1) and this pictorial representation of the world occurs in and through language. Language is composed of words constructed in the form of sentences, and if sentences assert the existence of "states of affairs" they are "the simplest kind of proposition, an elementary proposition" (4.21) and, as simplest, they constitute a mirror image of reality at its most ultimate. (It should perhaps be noted that the precise nature of an "elementary proposition" is left inchoate in the *Tractatus* and is highly disputed in the secondary literature.)

From a synoptic point of view, "The totality of true thoughts is a picture of the world" (3.01) and here philosophy as a sort of therapeutics comes upon the scene. For it is Wittgenstein's belief that "language disguises thoughts" (4.002), especially everyday language which "is a part of the human organism and is no less complicated than it" (4.002). Wittgenstein then infers that "the object of philosophy is the logical clarification of thoughts" (4.112). Most of the problems that puzzled philosophers, Wittgenstein contends, are illusory and arose because those of a reflective bent did not understand the logic of the language in which they were carrying on their normal linguistic activities, especially when they attempted to employ this same language on such inherently murky matters as motion and rest, identity and difference, and the like. The young Wittgenstein concluded that what "can be said" with most confidence are "the propositions of natural sciences" (6.53). And given the additional fact that "logic pervades the world" to such an extent that "the limits of the world are also its limits" (5.61), there is also much which "cannot be said"—the pseudo-problems of classical philosophy on the one hand and the way in which the most plebeian fact about the world displays its logical form on the other.

Such was Wittgenstein's position around 1920. However, the next decade saw him grow disenchanted with what he gradually recognized as an overly simplistic account of the complexities of language and he began to sketch the short studies which were later to become the *Philosophical Investigations* (1953). Consider the following as a representative passage of his change of heart toward language:

> But how many kinds of sentence are there? Say assertion, question, and command?—There are *countless* kinds: countless different kinds of use of what we call "symbols," "words," "sentences." And this multiplicity is not something fixed, given once for all; but new types of language, new language-games, as we may say, come into existence, and others become obsolete and get forgotten.[2]

For our purposes, the key element in this passage is the introduction of the notion of a "language-game." Wittgenstein then describes the notion: "The term 'language-*game*' is meant to bring into prominence the fact that the *speaking* of language is part of an activity, or of a form of life" (sec. 23). Thus the notion of a game carries with it the notion of rules; and just as there are numerous types of games, each with its own set of rules, there are also countless types of language-games, each—and this is of crucial importance for unraveling philosophical tangles—with its own set of rules determining when the game can be played meaningfully and when not.

What are some typical games? Wittgenstein lists a few, among them asserting, questioning, reporting, speculating, making jokes, asking, thinking, praying, cursing (sec. 23). With such a diverse array of utterances in tow, Wittgenstein cautions that we can never know in advance what a word will mean in a new context: "One cannot guess how a word functions: one has to *look at* its use and learn from that" (sec. 340). Linguistic nonsense, which may eventually mean philosophical nonsense as well, springs from confusing the rules of one language-game with those of another. A rule, for Wittgenstein, is characterized as follows:

> It is not possible that there should have been only one occasion on which someone obeyed a rule. It is not possible that there should have been only one occasion on which a report was made, an order given or understood; and so on.—To obey a rule, to make a report, to give an order, to play a game of chess, are *customs* (uses, institutions). (Sec. 199)

And since there is normally nothing ironclad about obeying "customs," there is also a certain amount of leeway in abiding by the rules of a language-game:

> For how is the concept of a game bounded? What still counts as a game and what no longer does? Can you give the boundary? No. You can *draw* one; for none has so far been drawn.
>
> (Sec. 68)

For example, there are no "rules for how high one throws the ball in tennis, or how hard; yet tennis is a game for all that and has rules too" (sec. 68).

Yet rules are flexible only to a certain point, since "there is a way of grasping a rule which is *not* an *interpretation*, but which is exhibited in what we call 'obeying the rule' and 'going against it' in actual cases" (sec. 201). Any language-game necessarily involves *some* rules in order to be a meaningful game and this is the point Wittgenstein intends to emphasize when he speaks of grasping the rule without putting an interpretation on it. To use that particular game in the actual contexts of real life, whether appropriately or otherwise, is simply to "grasp the rule." We can see here the importance of a context circumscribing each linguistic event, indeed of a component even more stable and, as one might put it, even more metaphysically intricate. For Wittgenstein contends that grounding each language-game is an element or elements which cannot be reduced to the inherent variability of custom: "What has to be accepted, the given is—so one could say—*forms of life*" (part II, 226, emphasis in original). Thus, in order to recognize how the fact of language relates to the complexity of factors constituting forms of life, we must minutely observe the human animal in its many activities and responses to its surroundings.

Wittgenstein's reasons for shifting between the definition of language in the *Tractatus* and its characterizations in the *Philosophical Investigations* suggest several illuminating ways to appreciate the linguistic subtleties in the twists and turns of Joycean prose. We have noted Joyce's device of coining single words for a variety of metaphysical pluralities—entity/entity, entity/process, entity/property, property/property. Such words, taken individually, would doubtless instantiate a number of distinct contexts and thus, for Wittgenstein, be related to an equally diverse number of forms of life. But there is a more incisive interpretation, assuming that the uniformity of individual words bespeaks a related uniformity in the forms of life themselves. Since diversity in linguistic form can become unitary—a possibility realized in Joyce's early style—there may also be the more abstract metaphysical possibility that at least some elements in even the most disparate forms of life might also be evocable as universals of some sort. In short, the form of language (that is, in *Portrait*) may play a part in revealing essential factors about the underlying structure of the forms of life grounding all language.

Other passages in *Portrait* yield more immediately evident results when examined from Wittgenstein's point of view. In the first chapter, for example, Stephen observes the prefect of studies Father Dolan who is about to punish him: "Stephen lifted his eyes in wonder and saw for a moment Father Dolan's whitegrey not young face, his baldy whitegrey head with fluff at the sides of it, the steel rims of his spectacles and his no-coloured eyes looking through the glasses" (50). Here also is an unusual ensemble of words—"whitegrey," "not young," and "no-coloured." Joyce sees the priest as primarily a pathetic figure, riddled with contradiction and nonbeing. Note the tension implicit in the combination of adjectives "white" and "grey" into one word—"whitegrey"; also, the man is not "old" but rather "not young," his eyes not "washed out" but "no-coloured." Joyce has made us experience the flaws and emptiness in the priest by introducing simple negatives along with simple adjectives to form not so simple compounds—a tactic again hinting at the much more radical reconstruction of language that is to come.

Wittgenstein has argued that in every language-game "to obey a rule" is only a "custom," and that the boundary of a game cannot be "given" in an a priori sense but can be "drawn." These dicta help to explain the possibility and insight in such stylistic inventions as "moocow" and "no-coloured." For though the relation between word and thing is complex and often mysterious, it is (if Wittgenstein is correct) at least true to say that it is very fluid. In the case at hand, Joyce ceased to abide by the custom of separating the entity from one of its functions and instead drew a new boundary, generating a verbal form which introduced the vocal activity of the animal *before* the term which customarily specified what will produce this particular sound—"moocow" instead of simply "the cow moos," or something of the sort. Underlying this locution is "the given" or the "form of life," with the crucial proviso that language may absorb the given in an indefinitely large number of ways, ways that include what is perhaps the most striking aspect of a cow to youthful ears. The possibilities are of course endless—the form of life might even be the *absence* of life ("no-coloured," "not young"), a negativity brought out by emphasis on nothingness and its cognates.

Wittgenstein's conceptual triad of custom, boundary, and form of life carry similar explanatory weight when, instead of fine-grained analysis of single words or phrases, they are applied to stylistic packets in Joyce's later work. From the first "Yes" to the final "I will Yes" there occurs a form of life unique in the annals of literature, Molly's great yea-saying to the Heraclitean onrush of this, that, and everything else. One first notes the omission of the customary punctuation, a first interpretive step toward reconciling life as lived with the way one might write about a reverie of this sort. The vivacity of Molly's soliloquy, especially after a day fraught with womanly chores, is an unusually volatile "given," a quality emphasized by the fact that many grammatical and customary literary "boundaries" are gently removed in order to allow her matriarchal and climactic charm to shine forth in all its resplendency.

There are many other relevent instances. When Bloom is stumping for the publication of an advertisement, Joyce punctuates the narrative with snippets of the prose often found in the headlines of newspapers—the effect is that the wind of daily journalism mirrors the real wind of the corresponding Homeric episode, with the larger than usual type an attempt to capture the literary potpourri of a newspaper headline. This representation offers an especially intriguing new boundary. Anyone who has spent time in a large city will verify that the headlines of the different papers published at different times during the day provide a certain measure of linguistic excitement. Literary custom has dictated that the size of the print is not relevant to the total meaning of what is printed in the text; but the activity of walking along a city street can be approximated, in some small degree, by representing in print the experience of confronting a series of newspaper headlines. Joyce accomplishes this by using visual effects in order to shake up our conventional reaction to and disregard of the power latent in the blackness and shape of print. The successive deadpanners who bore the signs "K.M.A." and "K.M.R.I.A." in the cinema version of *Ulysses* made this point in a delightfully double way.

According to Wittgenstein, articulated language becomes meaningful according to certain rules, just as games are ordered by rules. Hence his concept, "language-games." However, games are often played for no other purpose than for sheer relaxation or amusement, a qualification which is not prominent in Wittgenstein's thinking (although linguistic events such as word-games are obvious instances of activities both rule-bound and recreational). Now the playful aspect of *Wake* language is apparent to even the most cursory reader. And as a matter of fact, these two aspects of a game—determination of order by rules and sheer joyousness in the activity for its own sake—nonetheless begin to merge when the language of the *Wake* is sympathetically interpreted as a Wittgensteinian language-game. It becomes evident that the playful aspect of the *Wake*'s language depends to a considerable degree on its distance from the rules according to which the complex structure of that language is based. However, determining precisely how *Wake* language has become distant from these rules may eventually take us beyond the stated Wittgensteinian perspectives on language.

As we have seen, the rules structuring the generation of meaning in a language-game originate as customs, that is, tacit agreements to obey certain conventions whenever we speak and refer to things and ideas in the affairs of life, routine and otherwise. Another kind of custom establishes the various literary forms and traditions as well. Now if the language of literature obeys such conventions, then the playfulness of *Wake* language is due in part to the fact that it has broken with the relatively stable customs of literary tradition—in content, choice of theme, the conventions of spelling, syllabic modification, and incorporation of foreign languages. But the notion of custom also carries with it the idea that a language-game, even one circumscribed by literary boundaries, cannot be private, that its rules are public, observed by some significant segment of the speaking populace. The question then arises whether *Wake* language can still be considered meaningful according to Wittgenstein's definition of a language-game if, at some point, the accessibility of that language fades into the private, convoluted imagination of its originator. The inner workings of the *Wake* must be made as visible as possible, even and perhaps especially because of its structural divergences from the customs of literary tradition. Thus the more that *Wake* language becomes susceptible to meaningful interpretation by semantic and referential study, the less it can be accused of exhibiting a form of self-defined privacy which, if undiminished, would render some sectors of the world of the *Wake* essentially impenetrable.

In addition to the public/private aspect of a language-game, the Wittgensteinian notion of custom also entails a certain measure of historical duration. As Wittgenstein has observed, a custom is not established by the single occurrence of a certain act or verbal expression. It must be repeated many times. Now surely the same character of repetitiveness must obtain in order that the stylistic structure of a literary genre or type can establish a mode of reality similar to that displayed by a language-game. We may then infer that the more the language of the *Wake* stands as unique by remaining undeveloped in subsequent literary creations, the less likely that such language can achieve a mode of existence accessible to ordinary literary interpretation. If *Wake* language had generated a development approaching the level of a literary custom, the resultant diversification would have widened the ways in which language can be viewed as meaningful within the relatively isolated cosmos of *Finnegans Wake* precisely because of the visible contrast between the original forms of *Wake* language as such and their subsequent literary development.

Since *Wake* language may be said to be characterized by a single literary style, it then seems plausible to correlate uniformity of style with the uniqueness of the language-game. We can ascribe uniformity to *Finnegans Wake* because its language depends formally, in some essential sense, on a coherent underlying metaphysical structure. Therefore, this metaphysics becomes one defined by the ultimate "givens" grounding the various experiential elements which animate the structure of *Wake* language itself. Now for Wittgenstein, the correspondingly ultimate "given" is what he has termed "forms of life," with the resulting types of language-games all deriving their respective structures from the individual characteristics of each given form of life. Thus, in general, variations in linguistic custom will depend on variations in the form of life conveyed through language. For example, dreaming as a form of life will entail different rules for its linguistic expression from the rules appropriate for representing, for example, a perceptual act or an erotic experience.

Once we have assumed that a single literary style exemplifies a single language-game, the subsequent attempt to determine the precise relation between the *Wake*'s style and Wittgenstein's language-game will raise certain problems concerning basic presuppositions in both these approaches to language. For example, this correlation suggests that we question whether the apparent differences in *Wake* style (as between customary literary prose and the puns) indicate different language-games (our initial assumption thus being both naive and incorrect), or whether they are merely variations on, or different aspects of, the same language-game. From Wittgenstein's perspective, the answer depends on whether or not more than one form of life is present. For if there are many forms of life and if each form has its own distinctive language-game—and a suitable literary counterpart for that game—then *Finnegans Wake* will fail to preserve this difference if its uniform style reduces to a single language-game. The point here is not that Joyce the writer of literary language should be understood as in some sense beholden to Wittgenstein the philosopher of language. What may be learned from this comparison is, rather, that a certain tension may and probably will result if a single literary style must be stretched, perhaps to a point beyond its expressive capacities, to evoke various forms of life. Even from within the relatively subdued metaphysical phase defined by Wittgenstein's thought, a clash arises when, with Joyce in view, one compares linguistic style marked by an identity of form with diversified subject matter.

Part I attempted to show in some detail that the unanimity of style in the *Wake* depends to a considerable degree on the structural details of its underlying metaphysics. At this point one essential difference between Joyce and Wittgenstein emerges regarding a fundamental understanding of language. Even someone sympathetic to the Wittgenstein approach could contend in the face of Wittgenstein's necessary plurality of language-games that the scope and detail of *Wake* metaphysics is sufficiently universal to accommodate all of Wittgenstein's forms of life, however many and individually complex they may be. Furthermore, whatever linguistic devices would be needed to obey the rules generated by the diversity of forms of life are all contained—perhaps *embedded* is more descriptively apt—within the thick textures of the *Wake*'s language.

Wittgenstein does not develop his concept of the form of life in anything like an explicitly metaphysical framework, at least not in the texts comprising the *Philosophical Investigations*. Wittgenstein himself apparently felt that the notion was either sufficiently specific as stated, or that the attempt to speculate about a metaphysical structure which was intended to span the common elements of most or all possible forms of life was futile. Assuming, however, that we give the Joycean challenge a hearing, the questions it raises must be resolved within the domain of metaphysics. For if the follower of Wittgenstein were to assert that *Wake* language has been drawn from more than one form of life, then the burden would be on the Wittgensteinian to show why the *Wake* cannot be understood as a single—if very complex—form of life. The Joycean seems justified in claiming that the *Wake*'s unified vision of metaphysical flux constitutes one form of life, a form endowed with a variety of perspectives, elements, and modes of articulation. To refute this interpretation by pointing to different forms of life within the *Wake*'s language, the Wittgensteinian must be willing to take a stand on what distinguishes one form of life from another, an issue which inevitably will bring nonlinguistic factors into play. Thus if perceiving while awake and perceiving while dreaming are in some respects qualitatively different forms of life, then the difference between them depends on features pertaining to waking perception which do not characterize dreaming perception—and not just on language about waking perception versus language about dreaming perception.

Wittgenstein broaches the notion of a language-game so that it appears metaphysically neutral. Yet it seems that the extent to which it depends on the logically prior notion of a form of life is the extent to which a language-game becomes no less metaphysically saturated and defined than is the literary structure of *Finnegans Wake*. For all of Wittgenstein's care in analyzing the details of the many language-games considered in the *Philosophical Investigations*, the notion of a language-game itself lacks a fully developed metaphysical dimension possessed by that perhaps unique literary language-game which is the *Wake*. It is not that the *Wake*'s metaphysics is any more adequate than are Wittgenstein's forms of life as a strictly philosophical position on the nature of reality, or even that this metaphysics is adequate as the philosophical ground for the *Wake*'s own expansive literary panorama. It is simply that the language of the *Wake* has been formed so that it explicitly inhabits the metaphysical realm by positing a coherently structured abstract metaphysical whole which grounds the language contained in the work proper.

Wittgenstein's apparent reluctance to indulge in metaphysics —while concurrently claiming to have unearthed the particular structures of numerous language-games—can be taken as a quasi-metaphysical position, that is, that such excursions into the ethereal regions of speculative thinking are either impossible or unnecessary. But are they? The *Wake* would have us think metaphysically, and in the grand manner, about language and its relation to reality while in the very process of compelling us to struggle to understand the myriad details of this complex literary language. As we have seen, it is virtually impossible to avoid thinking philosophically to some degree even if all we want to achieve is a measure of literary comprehension of the *Wake.* In assuming that a confrontation between Joyce's *Wake* and Wittgenstein's *Philosophical Investigations* with respect to the relation between language and metaphysics represents a real philosophical possibility, we have learned to wonder whether what might be called the metaphysics of language stands for a matter of inquiry which can be pursued or ignored according to one's philosophical and literary tastes.

Husserl and Joyce

In an illuminating metaphor, Wittgenstein describes language as "a labyrinth of paths." He then elaborates: "You approach from *one* side and know your way about; you approach the same place from another side and no longer know your way about."[3] Presumably "the same place" refers to whatever forms of life may be approached by linguistic paths determined as distinct language-games. Now Edmund Husserl's thought is also concerned with what might be called "forms of life." For Husserl, however, the structure of these forms is subjected to considerably more metaphysical scrutiny and correlated with language from a much different perspective than that grounding Wittgenstein's position. The principal differences will become apparent in the course of the following outline.

At first glance, it may not be evident that Husserl's philosophical interests included the purely literary use of language. But Husserl was in fact so concerned, although in a somewhat oblique way. A connected statement of this concern can be pieced together from the program presented in his relatively early work entitled *Ideas: General Introduction to Pure*

Phenomenology.[4] There, for example, we meet this provocative passage: "Hence, if anyone loves a paradox, he can really say, and say with strict truth if he will allow for the ambiguity, that the element which makes up the life of phenomenology as of all eidetical science is 'fiction,' that fiction is the source whence the knowledge of 'eternal truths' draws its sustenance."[5] The care with which Husserl has constructed this claim should alert the reader that the precise nature of the "paradox" referred to is complex and not readily apparent because of its ambiguity. However, the general contours of the paradox can be briefly sketched within the context of truth and falsity—how can fiction in general and literature as a type of fiction in particular be neither true nor false in any of the customary philosophical senses, yet at the same time be "the source whence the knowledge of 'eternal truths' draws its sustenance"? The paradox is the conflict between the fantasy character of fiction as such and the truth claims made for fiction as part of the "life" of phenomenology.

But note that Husserl does not *equate* fiction with eternal truths—he asserts only that the former is the *source* of the latter. It is therefore perfectly possible for phenomenology as an 'eidetic science" to draw its nourishment from fictional sources in such a manner that the results, suitably modified, can then be expressed as true statements concerning real essences. For our purposes, the problem is to isolate and describe this source so that its role in relation to literary production becomes evident, particularly for the processes involved in fashioning anything like the complicated cosmology of the *Wake.*

As a prerequisite for answering this problem, we must briefly describe what, in general, Husserl intends his thinking to accomplish. To this end, we shall allow Husserl himself to speak as much as possible.

Husserl defines "pure or transcendental phenomenology" as "a science of essential Being" or, in short, an "eidetic" science (p. 40). What does Husserl mean by "Being"? In this technical sense, Being is "neither more nor less than that which we refer to on essential grounds as 'pure consciousness,' 'pure consciousness' with its pure 'correlates of consciousness' " . . . (p. 101). Pure consciousness originates from an ego existing in a state which Husserl designates as the natural attitude, that is, the individual human ego permeated by all the natural concerns of normal life. In *Ideas* and subsequent works, Husserl presents various accounts of the processes, or "reductions," necessary before the individual ego can be transformed into a dimension of consciousness capable of yielding results which can be described as pure. These accounts are all extremely intricate, and the significance of their details remains in dispute in the secondary literature. What is clear, however, is that the "Being" of anything always depends upon an appropriately reduced or purified consciousness of that thing, whatever type of thing it may be. Thus the consciousness streaming from the pure ego is the subject pole in necessary conjunction with that thing as such, while the objects intended by consciousness—the correlates of consciousness—constitute the object pole. And Husserl is at pains to emphasize that both poles are always present in the process of scientifically determining the nature of essences and our knowledge of them.

Husserl also insists that "an individual object is not simply and quite generally an individual," but rather "it has its own proper mode of being, its own supply of essential predicates which must qualify it" (p. 47). And, as an important metaphysical corollary, "Whatever belongs to the essence of the individual can also belong to another individual" until it is possible to delimit "regions" or "categories" of individuals (p. 47). Finally, these essences can be exemplified through "perception, memory, and so forth, but just as readily also in the mere data of fancy (*Phantasie*)" (p. 50). Thus if consciousness is concerned with the world of fancy through whatever products, literary or otherwise, may emerge from within that world, then the discovery of an eidetic essence is just as likely to occur there, in fancy, as in perception or any other type of consciousness.

Furthermore, the conditions required for the establishment and categorical description of an eidetic essence can be interpreted and applied to what transpires in the sphere of literary or fictive fancy as such. For Husserl, these essences are drawn from various types of consciousness interacting with one another, and fancy can perhaps best be approached as a mode of consciousness unique unto itself by comparing it with a more prevalent type of consciousness, perception. Husserl asserts:

> Every peception of a thing has such a zone of background intuitions (or background awareness, if "intuiting" already includes the state of being turned towards), and this also is a "conscious experience," or more briefly a "consciousness of" all indeed that in point of fact lies in the co-perceived objective "background." (P. 106)

In other words, the nature of perception finds every "thing" (understood in a very wide sense) with an ambient zone of perceptual possibilities. These possibilities are in fact only latently experienced, but in terms of the potential revelation contained in literary language, they lie "in back of" what our day-to-day language would announce as the most manifestly evident aspects of whatever was perceptually at hand. Husserl then observes that "a thing can be given only 'in one of its aspects' and that only means incompletely, in some sense or other imperfectly" (p. 124)—a thing given to consciousness is necessarily experienced perspectivally. However, instead of relegating this property to a region of purely personal viewpoints, of variations on "It's all how you look at it," Husserl contends that it is part of the complete *being* of a thing to possess zones of background intuitions which could be translated into actual perceptual experience and, in turn, into linguistic representations of those experiences.

The writer of prose fiction is, of course, a pivotal figure in reshaping our standardized and therefore somewhat narrow perceptions of beings by shuffling language in a fanciful way until a heretofore hidden perceptual perspective is opened up. How then, from the phenomenological standpoint, does the writer, and by extension the reader, "see" what is "there" to be seen? Husserl offers the germ of an explanation: "There are reasons why, in phenomenology as in all eidetic sciences, representations, or, to speak more accurately, free fancies, assume a privileged position over against perception" (p. 182). While a given perception is limited in the extent to which it can reveal the essence of a thing, a "free fancy" reinterpretation of that perception has, by comparison, few such restrictive limitations. It is thus open to the pursuer of an eidetic essence to vary freely the perceptual field through fanciful possibilities in order to discover whatever consciousness of that thing must essentially possess. Reflection then indicates that free fancy, a methodological prerequisite for the seeker of eidetic essences, is the imaginative writer's normal modus operandi, though most of the time the writer—in continual quest for the *mot juste*—is probably unaware of a procedural technique which the practicing phenomenologist must never forget.

A related form of that resilient openness so essential for the writer must also be found in the reader. Perhaps not as fully cognizant of the many possible permutations that each perception is heir to, the reader must nonetheless illustrate and complement the writer's perceptual horizon with an appropriately expanded sense of fancy. Once the literary work comes into existence and an audience has approached for purposes of understanding it, Husserl points to the fact that in such understanding "we have indeed a seeing," but not a kind of "self-evidence" in the ordinary meaning of the word (p. 353). But what grounds are there for assuming that such evidence is available for the kind of consciousness pertaining to the apprehension of literary works? Husserl assures us that "to every region and category of would-be objects corresponds phenomenologically not only a basic kind of meaning . . . but also . . . a basic type of primordial self-evidence" (pp. 356–57). And since a literary object can surely be taken as a representative of a distinctive region or category, we may then ask what factors must come into play when consciousness concerns the self-evidence of a literary work on the epic scale of *Finnegans Wake*.

As we have seen, the concept of the "pure Ego" is crucial for Husserl, since it is here that the synthesizing of all intentional data takes place, the result leading to that knowledge of essences sought by the phenomenologist. The pure Ego is marked by the characteristic of "free spontaneity and activity" which "consists in positing, positing on the strength of this or that, positing as an antecedent or a consequent, and so forth" (p. 315). Husserl is thinking of positing primarily in a logical or scientific sense, but it is the "and so forth" which becomes relevant for the consciousness of a literary work. For in the literary transition which fancy generates by linguistically formulating a corresponding perception there is, in Husserl's words, "a challenge to spontaneity" in which "there opens up a chasm which the pure Ego can cross only in the essentially new form of realizing action and *creation*" (p. 288, emphasis added). The problem of describing the distinctive self-evidence belonging to the consciousness of literary objects will depend to an essential degree on tracing how the free spontaneity of the Ego spans the separation between the given of the perceptual field and reseeing that field through the consciousness of fancy. But the relevant point for our purposes is that Husserl has acknowledged the inherent power of the Ego, the subject pole of consciousness, to contribute to the structure of essential knowledge by spontaneously creating products of fancy. It should be possible to connect in a mutually revealing way Husserl's discussion of the relation between the ego and creative fancy with that uniquely fanciful product of the Joycean ego which is the language of *Finnegans Wake.*

Like Joyce, but unlike Wittgenstein, Husserl articulates a complex metaphysical structure to describe the general features of reality as related to consciousness. It thus follows that language, insofar as it can be integrated within this metaphysics, will be rooted to something far more conceptually stable than, as for Wittgenstein, mere "custom." This shared concern for metaphysics and the place of language suggests that a locus for determining comparative similarities and differences between

Joyce and Husserl may be circumscribed primarily by the metaphysical dimension.

Once developed in full detail, the Husserlian metaphysics would naturally be much different, both in content and in scope, from that enunciated in the *Wake.* Different in content, because the complexity of the relations between consciousness and its myriad intentional objects is such that whatever essences and regional categories can be specified will require a depth of analysis probably transcending even the detail achieved by Husserl's own thought, and certainly stretching far beyond the distinctions present in the *Wake* such as motion/rest, and identity/difference. Different in scope, because the *Wake*'s metaphysics cannot establish any priority between consciousness and the objects of consciousness. I have argued that the intricate structure of the *Wake*'s metaphysics must be understood as applying to realms of reality more inclusive than merely dream consciousness. However, as some students of Joyce believe, this structure may have both its origin and efficacy solely within the amorphousness of that one peculiarly fluid type of consciousness. This interpretation would of course set *Wake* language and the single state of consciousness grounding that language at some distance from the Husserlian position. For Husserl, even the bare possibility that a metaphysical order derives from and pertains to a reality remaining somehow outside the full panoply of consciousness threatens to invert correct phenomenological procedure. Only if the structure of consciousness can be exhibited in all its intentional forms will it then become possible to articulate the various categories which constitute reality in its essential determinations within the phenomenal and intentional field.

Despite this crucial difference, the treatment of consciousness in the *Wake* is relevant to the more comprehensive Husserlian approach in a number of revealing ways. Thus the very predominance of one type of consciousness—that animating the world of dreams—necessarily filters the referential dimension of the Joycean metaphysics through consciousness as permeating everything which appears in that dimension. The proponent of Husserl's phenomenology would applaud the insight that reality depicted in language must include the consciousness of the objects referred to by that language. As just noted, however, the follower of Husserl would not fail to assert that dream consciousness is indeed only one type of consciousness, and by itself it could never stand as the sole defining medium through which a linguistic statement of reality must pass.

This point would tell against the apparently unilateral character of the *Wake*'s streaming consciousness if, in fact, that stream were exclusively defined by the coordinates of dream consciousness. But we have shown that the language of the *Wake* is not a mere linguistic mirror of dream consciousness, but rather incorporates the fluidity common to dreams for purposes of evoking a metaphysical vision of reality developed through traditional metaphysical concepts in which fluidity predominates. The complexity of this structure suggests that this one manifest type of consciousness may, as a unifying medium, contain elements of a variety of other types of consciousness. *Wake* language thus becomes a joint product of dreaming and the Joycean fancy for instilling in that language the dictates of the grand metaphysical foundation grounding all forms of consciousness. Such language plays an essential role in determining what would be the Joycean equivalent of an eidetic essence, since under this interpretation the contents of consciousness are derived from the processes of consciousness as played out in their totality.

Wake language has sufficient complexity in this respect to justify noting another relevant similarity, this one between the unity underlying distinguishable types of consciousness and the multiform linguistic network of language evoking or illustrating the presence and structure of these types of consciousness. We observe that the unity embodying the consciousness of the nameless narrator of the *Wake* runs parallel to Husserl's "pure Ego," the font from which the subject phase of all eidetic knowledge must flow. The variety of linguistic devices appearing in the *Wake* can then be attributed to the spontaneous intuition of a Joycean pure ego. And the variations in the structure of that ego's complex consciousness (attested to by the shifts in style within the *Wake*) are occasioned by the fact that it intends different objects in different ways. Furthermore, this difference in linguistic style indicates Joyce's implicit adherence to Husserl's principle that any type of consciousness is conditioned by the variation in its intended objects.

But although the Joycean equivalent of the pure Ego does exhibit a form of universality, when applied to the complex flux of experience that ego does not proceed through those methodological reductions required for deriving the type of universality Husserl hopes to express. For example, Husserl's pure Ego is allowed to exercise its free spontaneity in the realm of fancy without concern for violating any restrictions imposed by a preconceived metaphysical system. Husserl's methodology guarantees that all such systems, precisely because they have not been subjected to analysis vis-à-vis the nature of consciousness as such, are bracketed and then put aside before the pure Ego begins its quest for essential knowledge. Thus whereas nothing can be at rest in the world of the *Wake* by virtue of internal metaphysical fiat, Husserl's fancy can perfectly well intend an entity or type of entity at rest in order to determine how an eidetic essence has properties pertaining to rest as part of the phenomenological interpretation of that essence.

Although they are always related to elements of dream consciousness, the various types of consciousness flowing from the Joycean pure ego must originate—as does dream consciousness itself—from some form of perceptual data. Husserl's claim that background intuitions are present in every perceptual act accords neatly with this multiplicity, especially when these types of consciousness appear in a distinctively linguistic context. Just as close scrutiny of what appears to be present in and around the perceived object will reveal a sediment of perceptual detail, so the background associations in the referential and semantic dimensions of language become much more evident as the layers of *Wake* puns gradually unfold their significance. The prevalence of these linguistic vehicles also illustrates the sense in which free fancy supercedes bare perception, that is, by compelling the referential function of language to multiply its members far beyond what would be typically perceived as the customary referent of a given word. For Joyce, language itself attests to the multiple texture of perception embedded in language; for Husserl, perceptual experience as such is essentially layered, with language denotatively reflecting that important property. Joyce demonstrates *through* language about perception what Husserl asserts *with* language about perceptual consciousness.

Finally, the variegated form of *Wake* language duly contributes to determining the nature of consciousness and the Joycean counterpart of essences derivable from applied phenomenological technique. *Wake* language would then, in its own way, illustrate Husserl's principle that each type of consciousness generates its own form of self-evidence. Thus whatever makes perceptual consciousness veridical will not be equivalent either in form or in content to whatever makes, say, the consciousness of memory yield accurate results. Assuming that the *Wake*'s complex depiction of consciousness can be approximated in some form or forms of actual experience, literary or otherwise, we should thus be prepared to seek the evidence for that approximation in a manner unique to the complexity of this experience, that is, in a manner not necessary assimilable to other types of consciousness in isolation. For example, that quality of dream consciousness relevant to determining the essence of objects and experiences referred to within dream consciousness must be derived from dream consciousness itself. But here a problem arises if, in fact, there is no other type of consciousness in the *Wake* from which to examine the processes and products of dream consciousness. For if consciousness in all its apparently distinct forms is directly reducible to simple dreaming, then it becomes virtually impossible to analyze that consciousness for purposes of distinguishing between what was essentially experienced and what was merely accidental.

To what could this type of consciousness appeal as evidence? How can a dreamer examine a dream while still dreaming that dream?

At this point, the follower of Husserl would perhaps repeat a principle already established during the methodological phase of the phenomenological enterprise. Although fancy has an advantage over perception in that it can freely vary the intentional objects in ways transcending the limits of perception, the pure Ego must nonetheless compare the results of such spontaneous variation with the more fixed data issuing from perception (as well as other types of consciousness) in order to complement whatever essential aspects have been provided by the fanciful yield of dream consciousness. And here we recognize that an important metaphysical reason why the language of the *Wake* is so difficult to relate to our customary forms of experience is precisely that the purely perceptual character of such language remains in the background, a mere supplement to the much more fluid form of perceiving proper to consciousness while dreaming of this and that. Even if, as I have argued, *Wake* language includes perceptual components of actual perception as such, it is still difficult for a reader—even one with some background in Husserlian principles and distinctions—to distinguish between the linguistic representations of dreaming and those of perceiving. The language of the *Wake* need not have been written with a view toward formulating anything like what Husserl terms eidetic essences in order to become subject to Husserl's principle that different types of conciousness must attest to the fact of their difference in different ways, even and especially if language representing all experience has been crafted in intimate alliance with the textures of experience themselves.

Another aspect of Husserl's phenomenology also raises pertinent questions concerning the potential relevance of metaphysics to a purely literary understanding of the *Wake.* After the appropriate data from the consciousness of particular objects and experiences has been gathered, Husserl posits the possibility of eliciting categories, or descriptions which cut across individual differences and which represent eidetic essences at progressively greater levels of universality. Now by comparison, notice that however complex the consciousness represented by *Wake* language may become, asserting a distinction between an individual character and a character type would be inconsistent with the *Wake*'s own principles. For once a given character assumes properties of a wider and more abstract mode of reality, this derivative form of universality, existing in a state of at least temporary fixity would conflict with the *Wake*'s contention that everything is in flux and that nothing remains the same as itself.

Most literary critics would agree that criticism should involve both the scrutiny of individual characters and overall formal considerations such as classifications as to type, genre, etc. In short, both particular and universal considerations must be applicable to the content of the work. But the difference between particular and universal is one of the distinctions which the content of *Wake* metaphysics explicitly denies. The possibility of such critical accessibility is, however, directly provided for by the diversity of Husserl's approach to consciousness and by the products of consciousness metaphysically derived from that approach. We must perhaps wonder whether the fact that literary criticism of the *Wake* is better served by the metaphysical foundations of Husserl's phenomenology than by more conventional criticism implies that the *Wake*'s doctrine of universal flux cannot do justice to that aspect of the flux which is the complexity of human consciousness. The point here is not that Joyce on consciousness must conform to Husserl's guidelines, just as Joycean language need not be compatible in all respects with the Wittgensteinian notion of a language-game. What may be worth thinking about, however, is that the metaphysical complexity of *Finnegans Wake* is such that it might require an interpretive approach based on an understanding of the relation between metaphysics and consciousness even more complex than that presented in the *Wake*, an understanding which Husserl's phenomenological program undoubtedly provides.

Conclusion

The similarities and differences sounded in this chapter partially indicate the extent to which the metaphysical aspects of Joyce's literary thought coincide with the ideas of Wittgenstein and Husserl as representatives of the vanguard of contemporary philosophy. The number of similarities is, I think, so significant that Joyce should perhaps be ranked as one of the most discerning literary philosophers of this century. However, can one make such an estimate if the work itself tells us that *Finnegans Wake* is just one mammoth "hoax"? By contrast to the great seriousness of Wittgenstein's and Husserl's investigations, does the surface puckishness of the *Wake* necessarily preclude the possibility that the work possesses a serious dimension? As I have argued, humorous writing in general and *Finnegans Wake* in particular may well be blended with its own kind of penetrating vision. And this potential alliance of wit and wisdom is more than sufficient reason to grant Joyce a hearing as an exemplar—or at least a literary reflection—of serious philosophical and metaphysical inquiry.

In fact, the many parallels between Joyce's fiction and the work of leading protagonists of contemporary philosophy might make us hesitate before bowing submissively to the idea that literature and philosophy are separated by distinct boundaries. One must wonder whether these particular humanistic products are, apart from well-entrenched academic classifications, really so different, at least to readers seeking a thorough understanding of their significance. Both Wittgenstein and Husserl are certainly much less literary in the expression of their respective philosophies than Joyce was philosophical in his fictional expression. If, however, I have demonstrated that approaching the literary Joyce on his own level requires a fair degree of philosophical training, then it may well be also that articulating the full ramifications of "professional" philosophers such as Wittgenstein or Husserl will require an equivalently sophisticated literary education, one which appears perhaps only in the thinking of a figure such as Joyce. This thesis is a natural outgrowth of the type of analysis we have followed, assuming of course that one approaches it from a suitably distant vantage point. But it also would require a lengthy and intricate argument, well stocked with a variety of literary and philosophical examples, to establish.

Therefore, readers may choose between two alternatives. Those who grant the possibility that the delicate interplay of influence described above is real will have received the impression that understanding the diverse humanistic expression of the contemporary Western spirit ultimately requires a journey toward a common source. However, others may adhere to the conviction that fundamentally irreducible differences separate the work of literary figures such as Joyce from the reflective utterances of their philosophical counterparts. But no matter which attitude governs one's state of mind, the fact remains that realizing all that is entailed in defining these differences, reconcilable or not, may be one significant benefit of a sustained reflection on the metaphysical elements in Joyce's major prose works.

Notes
Selected Bibliography
Index

Notes

Some Principles of Interpretation

1. Anthony Burgess, *ReJoyce* (New York: W. W. Norton, 1965), p. 264.

2. Compare Louis O. Mink in *A Finnegans Wake Gazeteer* (Bloomington: Indiana University Press, 1978), p. xiv, emphasis in original: "By now it is notorious that anyone who approaches the text of the *Wake* with some specialized subject in mind will not fail to discover endless allusions to that subject. Of course this occurs in part because some of those allusions *are* there, by any standard of objectivity. But in part, as one learns when one has observed the results of monomaniac exegesis, the phenomenon reflects the fact that the language of the *Wake* will anchor one end of any chain of associative meanings." Mink is doubtless correct in estimating the vast range of interpretive possibilities latent in *Wake* language. I would only suggest, however, that some associated meanings may be more helpful than others in controlling our understanding of how the *Wake* assumes significance. I appeal to the fifth of Clive Hart's six propositions for proper exegesis of the *Wake:* "The most important task of the explicator is to sort out the planes of meaning into an order of precedence" ("The Elephant in the Belly: Exegesis in *Finnegans Wake,*" in *A Wake Digest*, ed. Clive Hart and Fritz Senn [Sydney: Sydney University Press, 1968], p. 12). See also Hart's earlier appeal that critics of the *Wake* develop as few patterns of interpretation as possible: "*Finnegans Wake* in Perspective," in *James Joyce Today*, ed. Thomas F. Staley [Bloomington: Indiana University Press, 1966], pp. 135–65, esp. 157–65. My contention then is that the metaphysical plane, as developed in part I, ranks near or at the summit of the possible planes of meaning in the *Wake*, at least with respect to understanding its overall structure.

3. Thus Louis O. Mink: "The form of Vico's theory was useful to Joyce, but its truth was of no interest, and the relevance of Vico's great *Scienza Nuova* to Joyce's word-world is of exactly the same order as the list of Dublin's Mayors, or a list of Tom Moore's songs, which one scans in order to identify their occurrence in the text" ("Reading *Finnegans Wake,*" *Southern Humanities Review* 9 [1975]: 10). For the views of the principal philosophers present in the *Wake* (Vico, Nicholas of Cusa, and Bruno), see James S. Atherton, *The Books at the Wake* (New York: Viking Press, 1960), pp. 29–34, 35–37. And for a different perspective, see Hart, "Cyclic Form," in *Structure and Motif in Finnegans Wake* (Evanston, Ill.: Northwestern University Press, 1962), pp. 44–77.

4. See Adaline Glasheen, *A Census of Finnegans Wake,* 3rd ed. (Evanston, Ill.: Northwestern University Press, 1977). On the significance of Bruno in *Finnegans Wake* (although the conclusions in this study should be taken with caution), see Frances Motz Boldereff, *Hermes to His Son Thoth: Being Joyce's Use of Giordano Bruno in Finnegans Wake* (Woodward, Pa.: Classic Non-fiction Library, 1968); and Ronald J. Koch, "Giordano Bruno and *Finnegans Wake:* A New Look at Shaun's Objection to the 'Nolanus Theory,' " *James Joyce Quarterly* 9 (1971): 237–49. See also the discussion of the coincidence of opposites in Roland McHugh, *The Sigla of Finnegans Wake* (Austin: University of Texas Press, 1976), pp. 27–31.

5. Anthony Burgess, *Joysprick: An Introduction to the Language of James Joyce* (New York: Harcourt Brace, 1973), p. 10.

6. Burgess, *ReJoyce,* p. 182; subsequent quotations will be cited in the text. Burgess maintained substantially the same view in *Joysprick,* pp. 149–50.

7. Cf. Ruth von Phul, "Who Sleeps at Finnegans Wake?" *James Joyce Review* 1 (June 1957): 27–38; see also William York Tindall's conclusion (in apparent agreement with Burgess): "The *Wake,* then, would be the dream of Everyman or, since Joyce saw himself in this capacity, of James Joyce, a collective consciousness drawing upon a collective unconscious" (*A Reader's Guide to Finnegans Wake* [New York: Farrar, Strauss, and Giroux, 1969], p. 19). Edmund Wilson identified the dreamer as HCE but then insisted that "it is Joyce's further aim to create, through Earwicker's mythopoeic dream, a set of symbols even more general and basic." Wilson discusses tensions arising between taking the dreamer as an individual and what is dreamt as universal ("The Dream of H. C. Earwicker," in *The Wound and the Bow* [Boston: Houghton Mifflin, 1941], pp. 243–71, esp. 248–56). See also "The Dream Structure," in Hart, *Structure and Motif in Finnegans Wake,* pp. 78–108. For criticisms directed at reading the *Wake* as the dream of an individual dreamer, see Michael B. Begnal and Grace Eckley, *Narrator and Character in Finnegans Wake* (Lewisburg, Pa.: Bucknell University Press, 1975), pp. 22–26; Strother B. Purdy, "Mind Your Genderous: Toward a *Wake* Grammar," in *New Light on James Joyce from the Dublin Symposium,* ed. Fritz Senn (Bloomington: Indiana University Press, 1972), pp. 46–78; and Bernard Benstock, "L. Boom as Dreamer in *Finnegans Wake,*" *PMLA* 82 (1967): 91–97.

The Reality of Flux

1. Louis O. Mink, *A Finnegans Wake Gazetteer* (Bloomington: Indiana University Press, 1965), p. xi. For a more general account of the function of space, concentrating on *Ulysses* and those sections of the *Wake* available at the time, see Adelheid Obradovic, *Die Behandlung der Räumlichkeit im späteren Werk des James Joyce* (Würzburg: Konrad Triltsch, 1934).

The Flux of Language

1. See Strother B. Purdy, "Mind Your Genderous: Toward a *Wake* Grammar," in *New Light on James Joyce from the Dublin Symposium*, ed. Fritz Senn (Bloomington: Indiana University Press, 1977), esp. pp. 59–60.

2. Compare Henri Bergson's very different approach to the pun, for whom the "play upon words" makes us "think somehow of a negligence on the part of language, which, for the time being, seems to have forgotten its real function and now claims to accommodate things to itself instead of accommodating itself to things. And so the play upon words always betrays a momentary *lapse of attention* in language, and it is precisely on that account that it is amusing" (*Laughter: An Essay on the Meaning of the Comic*, trans. Cloudesley Brereton [London: Macmillan, 1911], p. 121, emphasis in original). See also Anthony Burgess, "Oneiroparonomastics," in *Joysprick: An Introduction to the Language of James Joyce* (New York: Harcourt Brace, 1973), pp. 135–61; and William York Tindall, "James Joyce and the Hermetic Tradition," *Journal of the History of Ideas* 15 (1954): 23–39.

3. Joyce was definitely aware of the importance of this Aristotelian principle. In the lecture on aesthetics to Lynch in *Portrait*, Stephen Dedalus observes, "Aristotle's entire system of philosophy rests upon his book of psychology and that, I think, rests on his statement that the same attribute cannot at the same time and in the same connection belong to and not belong to the same subject" (p. 208). For another interpretation, see Joseph Campbell and Henry Morton Robinson, *A Skeleton Key to Finnegans Wake* (New York: Viking Press, 1944), pp. 118–19, n. 18.

A Portrait of the Artist as a Young Man: The Forging of the Flux

1. Francis Russell, *Three Studies in 20th Century Obscurity* (Aldington, England: Hand and Flower Press, 1954), p. 44.

2. See Robert S. Ryf, *A New Approach to Joyce, The Portrait of the Artist as a Guidebook* (Berkeley and Los Angeles: University of California Press, 1962).

3. But compare K. E. Robinson, "The Stream of Consciousness Technique and the Structure of Joyce's *Portrait*," *James Joyce Quarterly* 9 (1971): 63–84.

Ulysses and the Fluidity of Consciousness

1. For an analysis of the language in *Ulysses* as based on more traditional rhetorical and stylistic categories, see Liisa Dahl, *Linguistic Features of the Stream-of-Consciousness Techniques of James Joyce, Virginia Woolf and Eugene O'Neill* (Turku, Finland: Turun Yliopisto, 1970), pp. 21–41.

2. A different metaphysical approach is developed by Therese Fischer in her *Bewusstseinsdarstellung im Werk von James Joyce von Dubliners zu Ulysses* (Frankfurt am Main: Athenäum-Verlag, 1973); see also Erwin R. Steinberg, *The Stream of Consciousness and Beyond in Ulysses* (Pittsburgh, Pa.: University of Pittsburgh Press, 1973), esp. "Simulating the Psychological Stream of Consciousness," pp. 36–61.

3. Stuart Gilbert, *James Joyce's Ulysses* (New York: Random House, 1952).

The Conflict Between Style and Reality

1. P. F. Strawson, *Introduction to Logical Theory* (London: Methuen, 1964), p. 3.

2. Martin Heidegger, *Logik: Die Frage nach der Wahrheit* (Frankfurt am Main: Vittorio Klostermann, 1976), p. 23; and *Nietzsche I* (Pfullingen: Günther Neske, 1961), p. 601, my translations.

3. Heidegger's thought has already been applied to such a purpose. In *The Decentered Universe of Finnegans Wake: A Structuralist Analysis* (Baltimore: Johns Hopkins University Press, 1974), Margot Norris employs her understanding of Heidegger, in particular, *Sein und Zeit* (1927), as a conceptual backdrop for her structuralist interpretation of the *Wake;* see esp pp. 73–97.

Joycean Language and Contemporary Philosophy

1. Ludwig Wittgenstein, *Tractatus Logico-Philosophicus,* trans. D. F. Pears and B. F. McGuinness (New York: Humanities Press, 1961). The book is divided into seven central themes, numbered 1 to 7. Comments on these themes are numbered 1.1, 1.2, 2.1, 3.1, etc. Comments on the comments 1.11, 1.12, etc. I will normally use this form of reference in the text.

2. Ludwig Wittgenstein, *Philosophical Investigations,* trans. G. E. M. Anscombe (New York: Macmillan, 1958), sec. 11. Hereafter, section numbers will be cited in the text.

3. Ibid., sec. 203, emphasis in original.

4. Some introductory work has already been done in comparing Joyce and Husserl. See Juan David Garcia Bacca, "E. Husserl and J. Joyce. Theory and Practice of the Phenomenological Attitude," *Philosophy and Phenomenological Research* 9 (1949): 588–94; and Rudd Fleming, "Dramatic Involution: Tate, Husserl, and Joyce," *Sewanee Review* 60 (1952): 445–64.

5. Edmund Husserl, *Ideas: General Introduction to Pure Phenomenology,* trans. W. R. Boyce Gibson (New York: Collier, 1962), p. 184. Subsequent references are cited in the text; Husserl's italics have been eliminated, whereas I have sometimes added emphasis.

Selected Bibliography

Adams, Robert Martin. *Afterjoyce: Studies in Fiction after Ulysses.* New York: Oxford University Press, 1977.

Atherton, James S. *The Books at the Wake.* New York: Viking Press, 1960.

Bacca, Juan David Garcia. "E. Husserl and J. Joyce. Theory and Practice of the Phenomenological Attitude." *Philosophy and Phenomenological Research* 9 (1949): 588–94.

Beckett, Samuel, et al. *Our Exagmination round his Factification for Incamination of Work in Progress.* Norfolk, Conn.: New Directions, 1962.

Begnal, Michael H., and Grace Eckley. *Narrator and Character in Finnegans Wake.* Lewisburg, Pa.: Bucknell University Press, 1975.

Begnal, Michael H., and Fritz Senn, eds. *A Conceptual Guide to Finnegans Wake.* University Park: Pennsylvania State University Press, 1974.

Benstock, Bernard. *Joyce-Again's Wake: An Analysis of Finnegans Wake.* Seattle: University of Washington Press, 1965.

———. "L. Boom as Dreamer in *Finnegans Wake.*" *PMLA* 82 (1967): 91–97.

Bergson, Henri. *Laughter: An Essay on the Meaning of the Comic.* Trans. Cloudesley Brereton. London: Macmillan, 1911.

Boldereff, Frances Motz. *Hermes to his Son Thoth: Being Joyce's Use of Giordano Bruno in Finnegans Wake.* Woodward, Pa.: Classic Non-Fiction Library, 1968.

Bonheim, Helmut. *A Lexicon of the German in Finnegans Wake.* Berkeley: University of California Press, 1967.

Brennan, Joseph Gerard. *Three Philosophical Novelists: James Joyce, Andre Gide, Thomas Mann.* New York: Macmillan, 1964.

Burgess, Anthony. *Joysprick: An Introduction to the Language of James Joyce.* New York: Harcourt Brace, 1973.

———. *ReJoyce.* New York: W. W. Norton, 1965.

Campbell, Joseph, and Henry Morton Robinson. *A Skeleton Key to Finnegans Wake.* New York: Viking, 1944.

Connolly, Thomas E. *James Joyce's Scribbledehobble.* Evanston, Ill.: Northwestern University Press, 1961.

Dahl, Liisa. *Linguistic Features of the Stream-of-Consciousness Techniques of James Joyce, Virginia Woolf and Eugene O'Neill.* Turku, Finland: Turun Yliopisto, 1970.

Ellmann, Richard. *James Joyce.* New York: Oxford University Press, 1959.

Fischer, Therese. *Bewusstseinsdarstellung im Werk von James Joyce von Dubliners zu Ulysses.* Frankfurt am Main: Athenäum-Verlag, 1973.

Flemming, Rudd. "Dramatic Involution: Tate, Husserl, and Joyce." *Sewanee Review* 60 (1952): 445–64.

Gifford, Don, and Robert J. Seidman. *Notes for Joyce, an Annotation of James Joyce's Ulysses.* New York: E. P. Dutton, 1974.

Gilbert, Stuart. *James Joyce's Ulysses.* New York: Random House, 1952.

Glasheen, Adaline. *A Census of Finnegans Wake,* 3rd ed. Evanston, Ill.: Northwestern University Press, 1977.

Goldman, Arnold. *The Joyce Paradox; Form and Freedom in his Fiction.* London: Routledge and Kegan Paul, 1966.

Hart, Clive. *A Concordance to Finnegans Wake.* Minneapolis: University of Minnesota Press, 1963.

———. "The Elephant in the Belly: Exegesis of *Finnegans Wake.*" In *A Wake Digest,* ed. Clive Hart and Fritz Senn. Sydney: Sydney University Press, 1968, pp. 3–12.

———. "*Finnegans Wake* in Perspective." In *James Joyce Today,* ed. Thomas F. Staley. Bloomington: Indiana University Press, 1966, pp. 135–65.

———. *Structure and Motif in Finnegans Wake.* Evanston, Ill.: Northwestern University Press, 1962.

Heidegger, Martin. *Logik: Die Frage nach der Wahrheit.* Frankfurt am Main: Vittorio Klostermann, 1976.

———. *Nietzsche I.* Pfullingen: Günther Neske, 1961.

Hester, Marcus B. *The Meaning of Poetic Metaphor: An Analysis in the Light of Wittgenstein's Claim That Meaning is Use.* The Hague: Mouton, 1967.

Husserl, Edmund. *Ideas; General Introduction to Pure Phenomenology.* Trans. W. R. Boyce Gibson. New York: Collier, 1962.

Joyce, James. *Letters,* 3 vols. Ed. Stuart Gilbert and Richard Ellmann. New York: Viking, 1966.

Knuth, A. M. L. *The Wink of the Word: A Study of James Joyce's Phatic Communication.* Amsterdam: Rodopi, 1976.

Koch, Ronald J. "Giordano Bruno and *Finnegans Wake:* A New Look at Shaun's Objection to the 'Nolanus Theory.'" *James Joyce Quarterly* 9 (1971): 237–49.

Lewis, Wyndham. *Time and Western Man.* New York: Harcourt, Brace, 1928.

McHugh, Roland. *The Sigla of Finnegans Wake.* Austin: University of Texas Press, 1976.

Mink, Louis O. *A Finnegans Wake Gazetteer.* Bloomington: Indiana University Press, 1978.

______. "Reading *Finnegans Wake.*" *Southern Humanities Review* 9 (1975): 1–16.

Noon, William. *Joyce and Aquinas.* New Haven, Conn.: Yale University Press, 1957.

Norris, Margot. *The Decentered Universe of Finnegans Wake: A Structuralist Analysis.* Baltimore: Johns Hopkins University Press, 1974.

Obradovic, Adelheid. *Die Behandlung der Räumlichkeit im späteren Werk des James Joyce.* Würzburg: Konrad Triltsch, 1934.

O Hehir, Brendan. *A Gaelic Lexicon for Finnegans Wake.* Berkeley: University of California Press, 1967.

O Hehir, Brendan, and John M. Dillon. *A Classical Lexicon for Finnegans Wake.* Berkeley: University of California Press, 1977.

Phul, Ruth von. "Who Sleeps at Finnegans Wake?" *James Joyce Review* 1 (June 1957): 27–38.

Pitcher, George, ed. *Wittgenstein: The Philosophical Investigations.* Garden City, N.Y.: Doubleday, 1966.

Purdy, Strother B. "Mind your Genderous; toward a *Wake* Grammar." In *New Light on James Joyce from the Dublin Symposium,* ed. Fritz Senn. Bloomington: Indiana University Press, 1972, pp. 46–78.

Robinson, K. E. "The Stream of Consciousness Technique and the Structure of Joyce's *Portrait.*" *James Joyce Quarterly* 9 (1971): 63–84.

Russell, Francis. *Three Studies in 20th Century Obscurity.* Aldington, England: Hand and Flower Press, 1954.

Ryf, Robert S. *A New Approach to Joyce, the Portrait of the Artist as a Guidebook.* Berkeley and Los Angeles: University of California Press, 1962.

Schutte, William M., and Erwin R. Steinberg. "The Fictional Technique of *Ulysses.*" In *Approaches to Ulysses: Ten Essays,* ed. Thomas F. Staley and Bernard Benstock. Pittsburgh, Pa.: University of Pittsburgh Press, 1970, pp. 157–78.

Steinberg, Erwin R. "The Steady Monologue of the Interiors; the Pardonable Confusion." *James Joyce Quarterly* 6 (1969): 185–98.

______. *The Stream of Consciousness and Beyond in Ulysses.* Pittsburgh, Pa.: University of Pittsburgh Press, 1973.

Strawson, P. F. *Introduction to Logical Theory.* London: Methuen, 1964.

Tindall, William York. "James Joyce and the Hermetic Tradition." *Journal of the History of Ideas* 15 (1954): 23–39.

______. *A Reader's Guide to Finnegans Wake.* New York: Farrar, Straus and Giroux, 1969.

White, David A. "Husserl and the Poetic Consciousness." *The Personalist* 53 (1972): 408–24.

———. "The Labyrinth of Language: Joyce and Wittgenstein." *James Joyce Quarterly* 12 (1975): 294–304.

Wilson, Edmund. "The Dream of H. C. Earwicker." *The Wound and the Bow.* Boston: Houghton Mifflin, 1941, pp. 243–71.

Wittgenstein, Ludwig. *Philosophical Investigations.* Trans. G. E. M. Anscombe. New York: Macmillan, 1958.

———. *Tractatus Logico-Philosophicus.* Trans. D. F. Pears and B. F. McGuinness. New York: Humanities Press, 1961.

Index